# Thunder on the Left

# Thunder on the Left

*An Insider's Report on the Hijacking of the
Democratic Party*

**Gary Aldrich**

A Patrick Henry Center Publication
Fairfax, Virginia

## —Dedication—

For the many dedicated men and women who work in the conservative movement and for all those who lend them financial support, allowing these brave cultural warriors to continue the good fight.

# TABLE OF CONTENTS

# FOREWORD—
## by Bob Barr, Member of Congress, 1995-2003

> "...secure the Blessings of Liberty to ourselves and our Posterity..."

These words were written many years ago by the framers of our Constitution and continue to inspire Conservatives to fight a daily battle against liberalism. One such warrior in this battle is Gary Aldrich whose love of country compelled him to stand up against a corrupt president. Gary has a clear understanding of the Constitution and the freedoms guaranteed to us. He also understands why we need to fight so hard to maintain our liberties.

Gary courageously defended our liberties in 1996 by exposing the reckless abandon of the Clinton/Gore administration as it turned a blind eye to national security and put all Americans at risk. Now he steps forward to tell us the rest of the story!

The Clinton administration's approach to national security was an outrage. As a former congressman who was also privileged to be a Manager during Bill Clinton's impeachment, I had a front row seat to Clinton's abuses and incompetence. I know the damage done to national security during Clinton's eight years in office. The Hard-Left always uses the excuse that the Vast Right Wing was conspiring to bring Clinton down.

I continue to remind people that it wasn't Clinton's womanizing

xii    *Thunder on the Left*

that the American people—or we in the Congress—were concerned about. Rather, we had a president in office who lied under oath and put our lives on the line by not paying attention to the blatant national security problems that were facing us. Clinton was certainly distracted, but that had nothing to do with the Right Wing.

If Clinton was bold enough to lie to Ken Starr's federal Grand Jury about his activities, consider what else he might have lied about: dangerous deals with North Korea, for example, or the technology which allows the Chinese Army to target American cities with nuclear tipped missiles. Did the Clintons and their friends look the other way in return for campaign cash? Are these the type of people who are best fit to lead and protect us? Gary Aldrich doesn't think so, and neither do I.

In his book, Gary warns us that there is a powerful and dangerous force that has hijacked the Democratic Party—the Hard-Left—and they seem to have no respect for the precious foundation on which our country rests.

Anyone who knows even a little about me knows that I've had it with these Hard-Left zealots. I'm angered because I believe, like Gary, that the attacks on September 11, 2001, and the deaths of over 3,000 innocent Americans resulting from that day of horror, could have been prevented.

As Gary Aldrich proves in *Thunder on the Left*, September 11th happened because too many extreme liberal Democrats like Bill Clinton and Tom Daschle and Richard Gephardt and Robert Torricelli, weren't doing the jobs good citizens sent them to Washington to do. They were sent to the nation's capital to protect this country. They failed miserably because their Hard-Left agenda and their desire to maintain power were more important to them.

While I was a congressman representing the good people in Georgia, I always followed my principles and kept citizens' individuals liberties, such as their right to privacy, first and foremost and let the other chips fall where they may.

Why can't Hard-Left Democrats do the same? Each of us took a serious oath and made a promise to the American people that we would protect them, and that we would uphold the Constitution, including working "to secure the Blessings of Liberty" for those who we represent.

Instead, those on the Hard-Left made us and our children vulnerable…and we're still reaping the consequences of their failed paths and policies.

Seasoned investigators like Gary Aldrich have helped to uncover and expose the Hard-Left's mistakes and miscalculations. The evidence is clear and overwhelming, and we're in agreement: the Hard-Left is reckless and dangerous and we should do anything we can to keep them out of power.

Their time has been spent not ensuring domestic tranquility, but ensuring domestic vulnerability; not establishing justice, but establishing political correctness; not providing for the common defense, but providing positions for gays, lesbians and Wiccans in our military; not promoting the general welfare, but promoting education to your children about witchcraft, foreign cultures, and condoms; not securing your liberties, but securing their next election.

This is the dangerous truth, but they don't want you to know it.

The Hard-Left has been masquerading as a friend and champion of the working man and of the little guy for far too long. It's just a shameless lie. They've tried to lull us to sleep by convincing us that the real threat to America, to the greatest country on the face of this planet, is conservatism. The "Vast Right Wing" must be stopped, they claim.

Most Americans, and even a few Liberals, were awakened from their slumber on September 11th and finally recognized our frightening vulnerability. Something had gone seriously wrong. Gary Aldrich and some of us in Congress and in the national security community tried to warn of this increasing danger for years, but few would listen.

The majority of Americans understand the depth of that danger today, but what's really frightening is that most Hard-Left liberal Democrats have hardly changed their tune after the attacks of September 11th.

They still don't seem to get it, and that worries me. They seem to be more concerned with their own re-elections. They're afraid of President Bush's high approval ratings. It's almost as if they would be willing to trade more American lives just to make Bush look bad. Could members of the Hard-Left actually be that craven?

We're finally fighting terrorism like we should. Wherever terrorism exists, and especially when its openly threatening the national security of the United States, we should deal with it in a most serious and consistent manner. All those who harbor or assist terrorists are our enemies. That's where we need to keep our focus and our resources.

But let's not forget what's happening right here on our own soil, right in downtown Washington every day. Gary warns us that we are in a "fight for the heart and soul of our nation." He's right. And, until the people of this great nation get wise to the dangerous agenda of Hard-Left liberal Democrats, we will continue to be a nation at risk as we drift closer toward Socialism and the ultimate loss of the liberties we know and enjoy today.

We need more honest Conservatives to echo the claims Gary makes in his revealing book—that the Hard-Left is dangerous, and that they put our American values, our children, and our nation at risk.

We need more organizations like his Patrick Henry Center to stand watch against an ever-growing, ever-greedy federal government colossus. In times of war, many citizens tend to naively, even willingly, give up their basic rights in exchange for promises of security made by their governments. This is a trade-off we do not need to make, nor should we allow it. We must stand with those like Gary Aldrich to curb the mindless growth of government and make certain that the seemingly insatiable appetite of federal bureaucracy stops reaching unnecessarily into our schools, our homes, our emails, our pockets, and even our SUVs!

Ronald Reagan warned us years ago that, "When those who are governed do too little, those who govern can—and often will—do too much." The responsibility rests on our shoulders to hold the leash of government tightly, so the government doesn't grow even more out of control. It's very difficult, if not impossible, to regain those liberties taken from us by the government. Republican leadership is better than the alternative, but too many Republicans seem unable, or unwilling, to rock the boat. The point is we can, and must, fight terrorism with the laws already on the books.

We must remember, Republican or Democrat, we desire power, and the "dark side" tempts some to abuse newly given tools of enforcement and security. Moreover, consider the state of affairs when one such as Hillary Clinton might seize the presidential levers of power. The picture is a dismal one and should give long pause to all who cherish liberty.

We must carefully balance our freedoms with our security now in order to guarantee that our children have lives filled with the same freedoms that our Founding Fathers set forth in the Constitution.

The Hard-Left is not just damaging national security, our precious children are being indoctrinated in the public schools by so-called experts who control our educational institutions with a zealous, almost hysterical, jealousy. They even think they are more important than parents!

What is now bred in our schools is a disdain for the God of our Founding Fathers. The Hard-Left continually attacks the Founders' character and morality, the Constitution, the Bill of Rights, the Declaration of Independence, and the Pledge of Allegiance. Too often, they even disregard the lives that were lost fighting for our liberty.

We ought to be concerned, and we have a right to be frightened by the damage that has been done just during the last few years of Bill and Hillary.

There are many ways to spread the word about the destructive agenda of the Hard-Left. The written word, particularly among those on the Right, is ever-increasing in popularity as a vehicle for conservative truth. Gary's books—especially when viewed in proper historical context—will be seen as serious warnings about what the Hard-Left is trying to do.

Further, unlike many others who try to warn us of dangerous trends, Gary has a unique credibility. He has the rare vantage point of an insider. He used his investigative expertise, gained from 26 years as an FBI agent, to investigate the Hard-Left from a different angle, from the other side of the fence. And I know from my close friendship with Gary, he tells the truth.

Seven years after the release of *Unlimited Access*, he blows the whistle again to reveal the Hard-Left's true identity and agenda. He warns us of its disastrous course and what awaits us if its advocates succeed. Gary reminds us that we must not turn a blind eye or underestimate this growing destructive political movement.

For decades we have been far too kind and polite to Left Wing extremists as they rip us to shreds with their scathing attacks and low blows. We must toughen up and stand firm against them—we shouldn't stoop to their caustic methods, but we do need to get thicker skins and not be afraid to jump into the fray.

We cannot allow ourselves to be lulled into complacency by those who falsely and quickly wrap themselves in the American Flag.

Don't get me wrong, we cannot and should not demonize all Democrats. We need a strong two-party political system. However, we must understand the Democratic Party is now ruled by the Hard-Left, not the "old school" Democrats who used to provide healthy opposition to the Republican Party and those whose patriotism could never be questioned.

We must be able to identify the Hard-Left and recognize its agenda. It doesn't have to consume our lives, but we should stay well-informed. Read conservative books like Gary's *Thunder on the Left,* get on the Internet for the latest news, listen to talk-radio, watch TV programming like Fox News Channel to get "fair and balanced" news. Learn your rights and defend them vigorously.

This is how you ensure for yourself and your posterity the Blessings of Liberty. We must do this—our lives and our precious liberty depend on it.

Gary Aldrich and I, and other conservative voices, will continue to spread the truth about the dangers of the Hard-Left's agenda and how we can beat them. Recall the inspirational words of one of our greatest American heroes, Patrick Henry. As this great patriot rallied our early leaders and our most humble citizens, Patrick Henry reminded them that, "we shall not fight our battles alone. There is a just God who presides over the destinies of nations, and who will raise up friends to fight our battles for us. The battle is not to the strong alone; it is to the vigilant, the active, the brave."

The Honorable Bob Barr
Member of Congress, 1995-2003

# INTRODUCTION—

"Extremism in defense of liberty is no vice. Tolerance in the face of tyranny is no virtue."          —Barry Goldwater

"Moderation in the face of the Hard-Left agenda is a dangerous folly or simple cowardice."     —Gary Aldrich

January 20, 2003, marked an important date for me. Exactly ten years before, a rag-tag tribe of passionate, true-blue Hard-Lefties entered the White House and began their destruction of the office of the president, our national security, and our American values. I was an eyewitness to their dangerous evils.

Just as they had bullied and bamboozled Washington political leaders during the radical Sixties when they turned our world upside down, in the nineties, the Hard-Left once again ran roughshod over D.C. and the nation as a whole.

Our slow learners, some still in power, scratch their heads, attempting to make sense of what happened during those eight horrible years. September 11, 2001, enlightened some, but others still don't get it—or at least they don't appear to.

Back in 1993, when I documented the presence of the Hard-Left as an FBI agent working in the White House and got a glimpse of their agenda, I tried to warn my superiors. I was certain, given that they were responsible for the maintenance of domestic and national security, that they would be gravely concerned. And yet, the FBI remained blind to the dangers of Bill and Hillary Clinton and their many Hard-Left conspiracies.

At that time, the FBI only seemed interested in maintaining a budget, fearing that Clinton would force massive cuts. Indeed, Clinton tried to cut the FBI's budget in spite of the friendly—even ingratiating—posturing of FBI bureaucrats. Thankfully, Congress overruled Clinton and restored the FBI's budget.

In contrast to Congress's swift protection of intelligence agency budgets, they moved like molasses on a cold day in January when it came to the many dangers the Hard-Left Clinton administration represented to our culture and our national security.

It's a fact that Clinton's like-minded political operatives monkey-wrenched national security safeguards in every important agency in the executive branch, right under the nose of Congress.

Many representatives and senators acted bewildered or unconcerned by what was clearly a mindless and gratuitous destruction of critical agencies. Still others wrongly believed this to be a momentary chaos occasioned by know-nothing hillbillies from a backward Southern state.

As I reflect on those years, I realize that there were but a precious few in Washington who understood the threat for what it really was.

Pundits, journalists, authors, educators and politicians also struggled to make sense of the corruptive activities flowing from 1600 Pennsylvania Avenue, but most missed the mark by a mile.

Common sense told the people of this nation what was really going on. That's why my book, *Unlimited Access: An FBI Agent Inside the Clinton White House,* about what I had learned as I worked behind enemy lines, shocked the nation but became a #1 *New York Times* bestseller.

I reported the truth about the Clinton White House, and the people instantly recognized the truth, as I knew they would.

After the book's success, I was immediately swept up into the opposing political movement. At first, I'm sure the Soft-Hearted Right liked having me around as exhibit A—I was proof of what they had been trying to tell the world about the Hard-Left.

The credibility and special status afforded me by the Right was due to my time inside the largest, most significant collection of this country's Hard-Left.

There were others who had tried in vain to warn us of the impending calamities that would rain down on this nation if the Hard-Left was allowed to continue on their dangerous path. But they were quickly dismissed by the mainstream media as scolds and cranks.

Their work was labeled as the highly subjective rants of hysterical Right Wing Conservatives. It didn't matter how well they documented their allegations or marshaled their facts.

Today, I call my new associates the Soft-Hearted Right because I have never worked around a nicer, more polite, more honest, more civil group of people since I helped collect dirty dishes after a Sunday church pot luck dinner.

I've lived and worked closely with this fine group ever since I emerged from behind enemy lines, and I've gotten to know them very well. For the past seven years I've continued my investigations of the Hard-Left, and I've also been able to observe members of the Soft-Hearted Right on a regular basis.

Members of the Soft-Hearted Right are the same adults who volunteer to become Boy Scout leaders, or run blood drives, or walk door-to-door collecting money for the Red Cross.

The Soft-Hearted Right are the ones who stand at attention when the flag is brought into the meeting room by the neighborhood firemen. They are the ones who become teary-eyed at the NASCAR race when their favorite country singer belts out the national anthem.

Take it from me: the Soft-Hearted Right are God-fearing, hardworking, patriotic citizens who love the Constitution, the Bill of Rights, and believe with all their hearts that what's written in The Declaration of Independence is absolutely true.

And the most ungenerous, intolerant, radical words they have to say to those who violently disagree with their beliefs is, "Why don't you behave yourselves and get some manners?"

That's what scares the living daylights out of the Hard-Left! Because if the Hard-Left was ever forced to behave like ladies and gentlemen, they'd have to give up lying about themselves and their agenda.

Without lying to their followers, the Hard-Left would find few to listen to their Socialistic rants about how the world will be a much better place when they're finally in charge of everyone's life!

If by some miracle the Hard-Left suddenly had manners, they'd no longer be able to scream and shout and talk over those who are objecting to their corruptive, failed, deadly ideology.

The Hard-Left will never behave, will always lie, and will never become mannerly. You'll never find real gentlemen or ladies in the Hard-left.

I now know precisely who the Hard-Left is and what they want. And the more I learn about them, the more convinced I am that they are dangerous to our country and our way of life.

I believe it's time for somebody to blow their cover, and I think I'm just the one to do it.

When I wrote my last book, I was aggressively interrogated, then criticized by an angry media that could not understand how I could work in the White House as an FBI agent and then write a bestseller.

Some of their discomfort came from their belief that only the liberal Bob Woodwards of the world are ever qualified to report what happens in the hallways of the West Wing.

The Hard-Left is determined to control the message by attacking people like me who tell the truth!

Those same media scolds are out there now, waiting to pounce on anybody who dares to break the mold. They'll attack any daring to write or talk about the current political dangers that face us. In short, they attack anybody who's not a Liberal.

Just ask Sean Hannity, Ann Coulter, Michael Savage, Michelle Malkin, Mona Charen, and G. Gordon Liddy, to name but a few.

They're Conservatives who've recently written bestselling books, each telling the dramatic truth from their unique perspectives. They are trying to warn us about the dangers we face from the Hard-Left.

But media elites hate them and describe them as "extremists" or "immoderate liars"—and that's the nicest thing they have to say about these modern-day patriots and their wonderful books.

The mainstream media won't dare address an obvious question: Why are people reading conservative books in record numbers?

They sneer, claiming that these books and their annoying authors are merely a fad, entertained and supported by ignorant people who wish they could go back to the way things were during the good old days.

Ladies and Gentlemen, they are talking about you.

The mainstream media is blinded by their obvious bias. I believe the majority of Americans—like you—are fed up with the dangerous agenda of the Hard-Left.

I believe you are becoming wise to the lies. I believe you are sick of the bullying. And I believe you're mad enough about what the Hard-Left has done to our country that you will continue to do more than merely cast votes in periodic elections.

I believe that you and the other soldiers in the vast army of the Soft-Hearted Right are energized and engaged in a way that this country has rarely seen.

You are organizing, marching, and calling your congressmen. And you're voting in the booths and also with your wallets as you support conservative organizations like The Patrick Henry Center.

You're mad as hell and you're not going to take it anymore! Am I right?

Alas, I fear that too often we're too soft-hearted. And while tolerance and forgiveness is virtuous, it also happens to be our Achilles' heel. We need to toughen up a bit.

And, we on the Soft-Hearted Right need to learn more about the Hard-Left if we're to defeat or better control this scourge.

If the Soft-Hearted Right wants to stop our country's drift toward deadly Socialism and repair the damage the Hard-Left has done to our culture, you'll need to better understand the nature of the enemy that you're up against.

When you study them, the first thing you'll discover is that the Hard-Left is not composed of liberal patriots, as some would have you believe.

No, the Hard-Left harbors a vicious hatred for our Traditional American Values, our flag, our Constitution, and a sneering hatred toward our faith in God.

The Hard-Left reflexively hates anything it cannot comprehend.

The Hard-Left consistently favors a Socialistic, Godless, one-world government—a strong omnipotent central government where average citizens have no real liberty, and where they, the Hard-Left, decide how lives shall be lived, and who gets and who gives.

If they ever prevail, the Hard-Left will get and my soft-hearted friends and I will be the givers.

That's because every single Socialistic government in the world has eventually turned its honest citizens into beasts of burden, into donkeys fit only to pull the carts of government.

Why, we wonder, don't they love liberty, as we do—as Patrick Henry and many other Founding Fathers envisioned it? Why are they so violently intolerant of freedom? Why are they so disturbed by those who want to worship God and have Him as a central part of their everyday lives, including—yes—even a part of the federal government?

Why does the Hard-Left even continue to exist? Why are these people so hard to defeat, and why can't we control them? Why is their influence felt so dramatically beyond what their puny numbers would suggest, especially when the general population of this country votes again and again to support and restore conservatism as our preferred way of living?

These are tough questions. No matter how much I study the Hard-Left, I'll never understand why some people live to destroy themselves and others. Why do they seem determined to ruin the best country on the face of this earth?

Why hasn't the resulting messy and deadly chaos they've created taught them that their way is always a predictable and regrettable failure, no matter how many times it's forced upon civilized people?

What I do know is that the Hard-Left has always been among us, and will probably always be a force, somewhere in the world, that we ignore or underestimate at our own peril.

Like the mythical Dracula, the Hard-Left can—from time to time—appear to be dead or dying. But we cannot be fooled for one moment! We must not let our soft, kind hearts drop our guard for even a second.

That's because what appears to be finished and at rest, can rise up to inflict a deadly wound when you least expect it. Take it from a former law enforcement officer.

Even when the Hard-Left is weakened, it is strong in ways that decent, honest people cannot even imagine.

With the mythical Dracula, there could be finality—a silver stake could be driven through its heart. If someone was courageous enough to do that—the story goes—the bloodsucking evil menace would never again threaten innocent adults and children.

There is no silver stake solution for what faces us. I believe a tougher stance and a harder heart is the only thing that stands between our nation as we love it, and eventual destruction forced upon us by the dangerously irrational armies of the Hard-Left.

.

# PART I

# PROFILE OF THE HARD-LEFT

# CHAPTER ONE—
# Hard-Left Loves Big Government

When President Bush appeared in Senator Daschle's home state of South Dakota on the occasion of the 75th anniversary of the dedication of Mount Rushmore, Hard-Left Senator Tom "Puff" Daschle used the opportunity to attack President Bush's plan to reorganize current federal agencies into a mega-agency to protect homeland security.

Daschle said he opposed President Bush's plan because he wanted to be sure federal workers couldn't be fired on the spot, but he never explained why they shouldn't be.

What's so holy about a federal worker? Why should these benefit-laden bureaucrats have special rights that none of the rest of us have? There are thousands and thousands of fresh college graduates standing in line to get those jobs. There's no shortage of good, honest, hardworking people to fill any vacancy in the federal government.

It's not true that the federal government has a hard time finding good people, but this worn-out myth is the only thing the Democrats can find as a reason why we must suffer from mediocrity in our federal agencies.

In his effort to pander to the union vote, Daschle walked right into a bear trap, suggesting mediocre performance from federal workers should be traded for national security.

But, this is a prime example of a classic tradeoff the Hard-Left has had to make—your security and my security for votes to keep Daschle and his Hard-Left buddies in power. Daschle attacked Bush because he needed to cater to one of the many special interest groups who own the Democratic Party. But if you accuse Daschle of being unpatriotic, moderates will scream in protest and accuse you of being too extreme.

Sadly, some of those moderates work for the other political party—the Republicans. They still don't understand that the other war we are fighting is for the heart and soul of our nation. The Hard-Left is taking us down the road to Socialism—or worse—and people are dying every day because of the Hard-Left's dangerous politics!

Fellow travelers and useful idiots who support Daschle and his leftist politics are quite willing to trade away your security, as long as they and their families are not affected.

Take it from me. I worked for the federal government for more than 30 years. I spent time in various federal agencies all over the country, and two truths emerged from that experience. First, there are thousands of selfish federal employees who can and should be fired "on the spot" for a lot of great reasons. One good reason is that in some cases there isn't enough work for them to do to justify continued employment.

Secondly—and this is the great irony—if the federal government actually fired thousands of federal workers on the spot, nobody would ever miss them, including their fed-up hardworking and honest coworkers!

You may correctly assume there are lots of good reasons for firing any number of federal employees. I would suggest a 25 percent cut in numbers of employees would only benefit the agencies and would allow hard working citizens to get some of their tax dollars back!

One day, while walking through the White House's New Executive Office Building—the "Taj Mahal" that houses the Office of Management and Budget—I noted that an assistant to an OMB senior manager, who should have known better, was enjoying a pleasant game of solitaire on her government-owned computer!

It was not lunchtime, nor was it her break time.

Her behavior stood out because this employee was not making any attempt to hide an obvious misuse of government time and property. She was by no means an exception. I witnessed dozens of incidents just like this over at the FBI and in the dozens of agencies that I visited on a regular basis. It would be shocking for decent, hardworking, tax-paying citizens to learn that some FBI agents are sitting around in squad rooms having long, deep discussions about the latest sale down at Macy's.

But it's true, and right now there isn't much that FBI managers can do about it.

I'm happy to report that most federal employees are repelled and disgusted by such open displays of total disregard for the mission of the agencies for which they work—but the fact that the manager's hands are tied from taking any real action against lazy, stupid or insolent employees is well-known to most seasoned federal employees. The ones who care have long accepted the fact that there are legions of federal employees who have drifted into patterns of incompetence and solid reluctance to do a day's work for a day's pay.

Couple that with a federal agency mentality that insists that certain numbers of this kind or that kind must be hired to meet diversity goals, and you have created a significant morale problem that infects the entire working group. Before long, it becomes obvious that the Human Resources department has cut corners to meet artificial goals, resulting in large numbers of employees who cannot perform the very tasks for which they were hired. This means that everyone else has to work harder to compensate for the incompetence of these workers. Otherwise, the work does not get done.

Making matters worse, the agencies have institutionalized diversity considerations in their promotional schemes. Good employees who have worked hard and are qualified for promotion based on merit, are passed over in deference to upper management's real fear they will be subjected to lawsuits from groups who have perceived grievances if they don't promote their minority quotas.

The federal government should be the best that it can be to protect us from further terrorist attacks. Thousands of federal employees know just how difficult excellence will be to achieve in view of the number of unqualified, disinterested or over-employed individuals who exist today only as speed bumps on the road to achievement and eventual success in Bush's War on Terrorism.

We *must* get rid of worthless federal employees!

Senator Daschle thinks we can have it both ways: we can keep the entire pile of deadwood in their present positions, and we can also win this War on Terrorism. Daschle is a Hard-Left Democrat. This, in and of itself, identifies him as one who has long since given up on the ideal that the federal government can be a celebration of highly educated, highly trained, highly motivated individuals existing for the purpose of performing public service for the safety and betterment of us all.

Instead, Daschle takes the dismal position that the federal government is an employment pool of people who will most likely vote for him and his friends at election time. Daschle is the worst kind of cynic.

Vice President Gore—it is said—lost his bid for the presidency because he believed he could attack the Second Amendment, counting on forgiveness from many for trying to take away their right to own and bear firearms. How wrong he turned out to be.

Senator Daschle now goes down the same path, assuming that all Democrats agree with his position that it's more important to protect so-called aggrieved groups or other individuals who have found a comfortable refuge for their lazy and insolent ways—and who are more likely to vote for Democrats in order to protect their cushy federal jobs—than to promote those who do the job best and whose work merits recognition and praise.

I'm willing to bet that most Americans—regardless of political stripe—strongly disagree with Daschle's low expectations for the federal employee workforce and will let him know how they feel during the next election cycle.

Meanwhile, "Bravo!" to President Bush for trying to give us a higher quality federal workforce. War on Terrorism or not, this is the right thing to do.

## Rush Limbaugh Beat Me to It

When I first heard of the Shadow Government, what stood out for me was the magic number 100. When Rush Limbaugh made the point that for a time, the federal government could provide basic services with just 100 people in charge, I thought, "Yes!" Here was Rush, telling 20 million people how bloated and inefficient the three million-person federal government had become.

Of course, no one is suggesting that the *entire* U.S. government can be staffed by only 100 people. But do we need three million?

Having an off-site emergency location for this Shadow Government and other federal employees is nothing new, in spite of Senator Daschle's claims to the contrary. When the FBI hired me in 1964, we were told that in case of a national emergency somebody would be in touch with us, and we might be ordered to drive to a secret location so the business of government could go on. That call never came, and eventually my career took me away from ground zero.

But if thousands of FBI agents knew about this secret Shadow Government since 1964, I would suggest that a seasoned U.S. senator would know a lot more.

Speaking of more, the very size of the federal government may be one of the biggest threats to national security that we face. The size and diverse missions of our intelligence agencies, including the FBI, make them incredibly difficult to manage. The U.S. Congress and the White House have used the FBI as a catch-all law enforcement agency for every Tom, Dick and Harry legislative fix—from peaceful protests of right-to-lifers at abortion clinics, to piles of dirt investigated because of their threat to the environment, to deadbeat dads who run out on child support.

FBI Agents who had been looking into the activities of real terrorists were improperly used to interview Christian churchgoers because they had shown up on a list of those who believe abortion is murder. Imagine two burly FBI agents showing up at your door because you simply exercised your Constitutional rights. But Janet Reno thought this was just fine, as long as she could assist the White House in demonizing those citizens whose opinions differed from their Hard-Left political agenda.

The agencies and their leaders are not blameless. In Washington, the name of the game is not the real mission of the agency, but how many budget enhancements you can get out of the present administration and Congress.

Each Washington manager understands that to grow is to provide more management slots. The higher you go, the more you get paid and the more power you accumulate. Careerism is rampant in the federal government because there are too many federal employees falling over themselves trying to find something meaningful, important or satisfying to do. Since there is such incredible redundancy, they turn to the only mission that still makes sense—getting ahead.

Lost in all of this is the real reason for the existence of these various federal agencies. On September 11, 2001, our federal government got a wake-up call of the most extreme kind, but those of us who have been posting warnings were not surprised—except maybe at the size and scope of the attack.

But it could have been even worse, considering we were not prepared.

Those who wanted to attack us were given everything but a red carpet to bomb the Twin Towers and the Pentagon, and they could have done a lot more to us because of the idiocy and time wasted in investigating Big Tobacco and peaceful abortion clinic protesters.

Misusing the assets of agencies like the FBI detracted from more important work. And, as we all know, it's very difficult to run a good foot race when your own obesity is weighing you down.

The federal government has become fat and petulant, but the Hard-Left loves it that way.

Somewhere between the magic number of 100 and the three million federal employees we currently have on the roster, is the correct and most efficient number to get us what we want. Maybe September 11 will serve some good purpose if it causes us to reconsider the role and size of the federal government. After all, isn't the first job of government to protect its own citizens?

## *Hooray, We All Agree!*

If enough of us continue to sound the alarm about Big Government perhaps those in leadership positions will listen.

The Brookings Institute, a think tank that busies itself with matters related to the performance of government institutions, has just released a 48-page report agreeing with the findings of our foundation, The Patrick Henry Center.

We have been laboring for years to bring attention to the sorry state of the federal workforce, including some of the more powerful agencies like the FBI. We said the FBI was in deep trouble. The facts are in—the FBI was in trouble, but they are getting better under the leadership of a new director and a new president.

Long before September 11, 2001, we were giving example after example of agencies that had lost their sense of mission and were struggling just to get federal employees to show up for work. It wasn't as if they were missing out on a paycheck if they were a no-show.

They got paid anyway.

Federal managers learned a long time ago, to their everlasting regret, that if they tried to take on rank-and-file federal employees and attempt to remove them from service, they needed to spend the majority of their work-time documenting poor performance to even get started on this mission impossible. Unions and lawyers and certain minorities who received favorable treatment managed to make it very unlikely that unsatisfactory federal employees could ever be eased out.

If managers devoted themselves to removal of just one poor employee, the rest of the employees suffered from the absence of good management. Managers had to choose—let the one get away with murder, so that they could give attention to the larger group—or gallop full tilt at the windmill, risking severe damage to their own careers.

And then, there were the lawsuits filed by the fired employees, sure to discourage any well-meaning manager from taking action in the best interest of the agency.

So, Brookings, after many hearings, many months of toil, and dozens—perhaps hundreds—of interviews, has concluded that the federal government is a mess and needs to be fixed...fast.

The lineup of professionals who were part of their commission is impressive. The former Clinton administration officials who made up the left side of the ledger do not detract from its findings, but one would not want to include *them* in the solution side of this enterprise if Brookings wants to maintain credibility.

After all, these same Hard-Left rascals thought Bill and Hillary Clinton were running the federal government just fine, thank you very much.

I will agree with the recommendations of Brookings to this extent: they want to bring merit back, and they want to measure performance. They also want better pay for higher-ups, and I'm OK with that, too.

But the one area I can really launch an argument with them is their wish that federal employees choose the federal government as their lifelong career.

I think this is a dumb idea. Federal employees suffer from burnout no matter how much money they get paid. The bureaucracy wears them out. It's as simple as that.

In fact, higher pay just encourages some deadwood to linger on and on.

Instead, I suggest a mid-career option. Send middle-aged federal bureaucrats out to be re-educated or trained for new private-sector careers so that new employees with fresh ideas can come in and bring energy, initiative, and other virtues that will guarantee high performance.

Also, if employees don't spend 30 years with an agency, the federal government won't have to suffer the huge retirement payout they currently face. This will lower the cost of government.

## Snow Job

I'm not sure when the GOP decided it was easier to sell tax cuts to the public than to hold the line on government growth. Could it have been at the same time that too many in the Republican Party decided they really do love Big Government?

I have to confess that I, too, was once drawn to Big Government. I worked for the FBI at a time when it was a highly respected agency that was granted whatever budget it asked for from the Congress just on the strength of a sterling reputation. The badge, the gun, the suit and the dark shades all contributed to an undeniably pleasurable power trip. Putting bad guys in jail for a living was just the frosting on the cake, and I never had to worry about unemployment.

Nevertheless, when I made my way around the hallways of the other federal agencies, conducting my investigations, I realized just how miserly our FBI budget really was. Marble floors and quality rugs, better furniture than I had in my own home, the latest computer equipment and decent office space in a nice neighborhood was not the usual environment for the average federal law enforcement agent.

But other federal bureaucrats routinely enjoyed these luxuries and much more.

We didn't get handsome expense accounts like some feds, but there was always the universal luxury of bloated personnel. There had to be, because nobody ever got fired. Enormous pools of do-nothing federal employees exist in every agency right now, and that means that the work which needs to be done may take two or more feds to accomplish it—one to work, and one or more to watch the worker.

Ask any honest federal employee and they will be happy to tell you this truth. After all, why should they hide the truth when they think nothing is ever going to be done about it?

You see, few political leaders will talk about a significant cut in federal employee ranks, but they will promise you a token tax cut. Are the American people too dumb to understand that even if they give you back a little of your money, they're going to spend it anyway? Republicans and Democrats alike feed at the trough of seemingly unlimited federal funds and few ever speak of downsizing.

Don't wait for agency heads to point out waste. It's been a long time since we've seen leadership of that kind in Washington. Who can blame administrators for being shy about mentioning the corruption, incompetence, and fraud? We've gotten so used to it, anybody who brings it up is deemed somehow odd.

And don't wait for the media to take up this apparently lost cause. The strength of the media these days actually resides in Washington, D.C. Reporting on state government is boring—besides, who wants to go to a state capital to have a party when you can be wined and dined by the President and his staff? Can you imagine a governor's office correspondence dinner? Please!

And yet, what is at the root of so many of our problems today? Ronald Reagan used to say that the federal government isn't the solution to problems—government is the problem! He knew that people were better off if they were able to keep more of their money. He also knew that so many of our problems were ones that individuals could solve themselves. Even when they could not solve their own problems, *local* governments were often in a better position to address the problem more efficiently, more effectively.

Today there is a federal solution to just about any problem you have. Fluff in your pillow? There are numerous agencies overseeing that. Water in your toilet? Rest assured we have several agencies on top of that problem. Leaky diapers? Don't fret—help is on the way! Relax and enjoy the comfort of knowing that a federal-nanny bureaucrat somewhere has a report on his or her desk that addresses your concern.

But what's the cost of this nanny-state we've created, and is it really in our collective best interest? Incrementally, our money and our liberties are being washed away, right down the drain with the bath soap that's been inspected by seven different agencies.

Of course, this suits those with a Hard-Left agenda just fine.

Just think—legions of healthy, happy, federal employees with too much time on their hands, just dying to snoop into your home, your car, your office, your bank accounts, your medical history, your bedroom— and especially, your wallet.

A Washington, D.C., winter sometimes includes heavy snowfalls. On these days, more than half the federal employees stay home because they don't want to get their toes chilly. Plus, they are not considered "essential"...indeed.

## Big Government Employees Agree!

I've been flooded with input from current and former federal workers who cannot believe Hard-Left Democrats would trade national security for organized union support and votes. Most of these emails confirm my conclusions that the federal government is fat with personnel, many of whom have become deadwood.

I'm speaking now of the stiff opposition to President Bush's plans to reorganize some 170,000 federal employees into one agency dedicated to Homeland Security. President Bush knows that a larger agency will give more cover to incompetent bureaucrats—and that's why he insists that he be given certain powers in personnel decisions. Specifically, he wants flexibility on hiring, firing, transferring and promoting federal employees.

It just makes sense. Federal workers who hold the public trust also have a hold on the future of the public safety. Whether it's a low-level mail boy or a mid-level secretary, each and every federal employee who is part of this unique group must perform at 100 percent or better in order to ensure national security during times of war.

For example, a single important document containing key facts needs to reach everybody on the routing list, without delay. Make no mistake—every piece of paper will be important because readers will make judgments based on the facts contained in these documents, judgments which will impact us all.

If a document sits too long on a desk because a federal employee is distracted, lazy, insolent, or comes back late from lunch, important, time-sensitive clues may not reach the proper parties.

Have we not just gone through sufficient examination of the FBI—an agency employing some of the most highly qualified, most motivated employees—and learned that agents could not get their memos read fast enough and were clueless about how to properly proceed with the information if they did read the memos? Their lack of performance brought into question the possibility that if the warning memos had been properly routed and read, maybe the events of September 11, 2001, could have been avoided—at least in part.

We'll never know, but one thing is certain: we're not paying people to sit around planning their next agency picnic or chatting about the latest Austin Powers movie—at least not right now. We cannot afford that kind of trivial misuse of public funds and public time.

But evidently the Democrats can. Liberal Democrats have gotten so bold as to appear in the courtyard of our sworn enemy and call our president a liar. I, for one, have no problem calling this traitorous. They claim that they understand the nature and gravity of the looming threat of more terrorist attacks, but if they did, how could they continue to insist that the federal government business be conducted as usual? How can they condemn President Bush's plans?

This position should raise a question: why can't Hard-Left Democrats get moving in the same direction as the folks who *do* know how to protect national security? Why won't they at least cooperate, even if they don't know how to do it for themselves? Why do they want to monkey-wrench the concepts of merit and excellence in the ranks of federal employees we depend on for protection? After all, it's in their personal best interests to have their homeland protected.

It would be one thing if Hard-Left Democrats would admit that they are unable to get organized and admit they find it too difficult to concentrate on matters of national security and foreign policy. Nevertheless, everybody knows Republicans are better at foreign policy and waging war. And yet, the Hard-Left Democrats will not defer. They inexplicably pretend they know how to do it. They do *not* know how to do it! The proof is in, and there is plenty of hard evidence!

There is no better place on the face of the globe to raise a family than right here; nowhere are people healthier, happier, more financially secure and more in charge of their own lives. 100 percent of us agree that it's a good life. That's why we still live here and millions of others are trying to move here! Isn't it vitally important to protect what we have?

So why would a Hard-Left Democrat fight with President Bush about making federal employees more accountable for their performance? Why can't they be subjected to the same standards private industry uses to ensure profitability? It's not as if we have to beg people to work for Uncle Sam—stacks of resumes stand as mute testimony that the very opposite is true.

The answer is simple but should disturb every American who loves his country: Hard-Left Democrats are simply hooked on power and the wealth that comes with it. Like a cocaine addict, they will lie and cheat to get their fix. They are so hooked that they will cross their fingers and hope they can buy time and get to where they want to go before the next thousands die, sacrificed to their greed.

Hard-Left Liberals seem willing to gamble that President Bush and his administration will work twice as hard to make up for the lazy, incompetent, and dim-witted who have managed to burrow into federal jobs. They may be right—and as long as we don't have another attack, they may be able to fight off Bush's plans to bring excellence back to at least some of the federal workforce.

But if they are wrong, we lose another mass of innocents to foreign terrorists because of a continuing incompetence in a workforce that's protected by unions and Hard-Left Liberals.

## *Three-Legged Race*

Everyone knows what a three-legged race is. Even if you haven't been to a picnic, you've seen television or movie versions of this funny event. A footrace is arranged, and just to make it interesting, two people are tied together at their legs with rope, and when the "go" signal is given, pairs of runners take off for the finish line trying to run with three legs.

Needless to say, it's very awkward going—many contestants fall down.

When I look back on my federal government employment, I recall many three-legged race occasions when I was teamed up with somebody who was unable—for a variety of reasons—to synchronize their behavior so that we could "win the race."

I'm sure that federal employees, current or former, can relate. President Bush is trying to do something about the lazy, incompetent, uncaring and corrupted federal employees we've acquired over the years, but he's meeting stiff resistance from the Democrats who claim that if a president is allowed to hire, fire, or promote federal employees on merit alone, we'll be headed back to the bad old days.

I have a message for the Gephardts and Daschles of the dangerous world we live in: These *are* the bad old days.

September 11, 2001, was the peak of the bad old days, and many mistakes leading up to that date were made by employees who were hired, and oftentimes promoted, for all the wrong reasons. A combination of affirmative action programs driven by hiring quotas, along with the installation of rigid, politically correct conditions, cemented in these employees for as long as they wish to be employed by the taxpayers.

Many statistics bear out my claim. It was recently reported that while more than 80,000 federal employees were found to be performing at an unacceptable level, only a few hundred could be separated from service. When a career in the federal government can be as long as 40 years, one can readily see how deadwood accumulates. And these days, too much deadwood is dangerous.

For those who claim that it should be hard for politicians to toss out employees for purely political reasons, I have one response: Billy Dale and the White House Travel Office.

One recent example of political abuse of federal employees on record was masterminded by Hillary Clinton, now a senator. She and her husband, Bill, not only publicly fired and humiliated Billy Dale and his entire staff—who had served many presidents well—but they called in the FBI and IRS to harass them, as well. Trying to cover up for their raw act of political abuse, they even tried to imprison Dale, but a savvy Washington jury tossed the case out in less than three hours of deliberation.

Are Hard-Left Democrats trying to save future federal employees from abuse by future democratic leaders? I would submit that instead of hobbling the entire executive branch with arcane and useless protections for do-nothing federal employees, they might take a lesson from Republican leaders who know not only how to maintain high morale, but also how to generate hard work and extreme loyalty from their staff.

It was widely reported that when Bill and Hillary Clinton finally left the White House, the permanent staff—who are among the federal employees that I'm talking about—cried with joy! That joy continued when George W. Bush and Laura, along with former President Bush and Barbara, walked back into the White House on January 20.

Now admittedly, down at the Department of Health and Human Services, there may have been some grumbling on the part of career employees who are dedicated to the cause of social programs on the federal level. But since George W. Bush has become president, not a single whistleblower from any of these touchy-feely agencies has come forward to complain about the way they've been treated. That's because they are being treated well.

With my 10 years of experience on Capitol Hill and at the White House, I can testify that the work environment created by Republican administrations is very good for the federal worker, whereas the opposite is true when the Hard-Left Democrats take over.

The truth needs no pretty party balloons to enhance its attractiveness, nor does the truth need snake oil salesmen like Gephardt or Daschle to help it along. The federal government is bloated with personnel, and many are not doing the jobs they are paid to do. President Bush is trying to ensure that federal employees who want to work are not handicapped like three-legged racers at a picnic.

## If It Ain't Broke…

After we were attacked on September 11, 2001, the population turned to the federal government for protection, and President Bush did not let us down. His administration has performed magnificently.

Nobody should be surprised since the federal government is doing what it was established to do, and it's doing it very well: protecting the population—the fundamental task of government.

People now trust the government in poll numbers not seen in many years. But when we're not at war, the federal government gets bored and starts looking around for matters in our personal and local lives to mess with.

It's not just the loss of liberty and the loss of money out of our paychecks that I'm referring to. A bloated central government breeds discontent in the population. Dislike for one's own government is not a good thing. People aren't happy when they dislike or distrust their own government.

But, people love the Constitution and Bill of Rights because of what these documents say and stand for. As a precursor, the Federalist Papers spelled out much of the thinking of the Founders as they struggled to get on paper a balanced form of government they believed would give us great lives and guarantee our safety and liberty.

One common thread running through these documents is the belief that the federal government should not be involved in local matters. An excellent example of local matters are our fire departments and rescue squads. The Founders had good reasons to conclude local matters should remain local.

First, they knew men of loftier concerns wouldn't be interested in local matters. They also knew that, from a distance, they could not possibly run local functions as well as residents of a community could. That's just common sense.

Alexander Hamilton wrote in Federalist Number 17 of another reason they did not want to meddle in local affairs such as law enforcement and the putting out of fires:

> There is one transcendent advantage belonging to province of the state governments, which alone suffices to place the matter in a clear and satisfactory light—I mean the ordinary administration of criminal and civil justice. This, of all others is the most powerful, most universal, and most attractive source of popular obedience and attachment. It is this which being the immediate and visible guardian of life and property, having its benefits and its terrors in constant activity before the public eye, regulating all those personal interests and familiar concerns to which the sensibility of individuals is more immediately awake, contributes more than any other circumstance to impressing upon the minds of the people affection, esteem, and reverence towards the government.

Now, I don't think anybody could argue that fire departments and rescue squads are not local activity. But the Bush administration is now calling them First Responders, trying to bring them into the federal tent by giving them funds, new assignments, and training which the administration claims is about new terror attacks.

But when the terror threat ebbs, will the feds still be playing with their new toy, the First Responders?

Does the federal government want to help the fire department? Fine. Give us our money back, and we'll give the necessary funds to the fire departments and rescue squads. They can tell us what they need, and we'll give them the money and any local law changes that may be necessary. We've always supported these groups, without exception—it's in our self-interest.

When called upon, they know exactly what to do, they have what they need, and they do exactly what we want them to do. After seeing them perform in New York and Washington, is there a single person who would claim they need assistance from Washington bureaucrats! God forbid! They sacrificed in a manner that has caused every American to sing the praises of these brave *local* men and women, and rightfully so!

So why is the Bush administration so eager to federalize something that clearly is working so well? Why are they trying to fix something that ain't broke? I like the Republican Party more when they behave as the party of smaller, less expensive and less intrusive government. The Hard-Left would be delighted to take over all government—local, county, state and federal. Let's never go down that road.

## *Third Party Emerging?*

I used to believe that in times of war—maybe *especially* in times of war—Republicans would have the clarity of purpose and the institutional knowledge of the Founders' intent to rise to the occasion and lead the nation to victory—without seriously curbing our liberties.

For years, Conservatives have been shouting that Hard-Left Liberals only want more power, want to create more rules for ordinary citizens and micromanage our lives—in favor of a Big Brother utopia. I thought

Republicans knew this and were fighting for our liberties, weighing every new law against the ultimate controlling legal authority—the Constitution and our precious Bill of Rights.

But I'm beginning to doubt that even if we prevail against the terrorists, the federal government we've built up to repel them with will not stand down, will not automatically reduce its presence in our lives, but will find support for the notion that these extraordinary intrusions we've rushed to embrace should be maintained just in case.

My fellow Conservatives have worked hard in the past to maintain and protect the country we love. During the Clinton years there was a sense that Bill Clinton and his cronies were not averse to using the power of the federal government against their political enemies. IRS audits of conservative foundations became routine, for example.

In fact, after the Democrats lost the House and Senate in 1994, the Clinton White House was convinced there was a conspiracy to undo Clinton's presidency, and they used White House resources to investigate those they considered to be the leaders of this emerging Vast Right Wing Conspiracy. They rationalized this abuse by deciding that any move against the administration could be considered a threat to national security.

Just as some say, "What's good for General Motors is good for the country," some actually believed that what was bad for Bill Clinton was bad for the country. Thus, any who attacked him, even for very good reasons, were considered the enemy.

Although many thought the Clinton White House's misuse of federal tax dollars was illegal activity, Congress didn't act aggressively enough to stop Clinton's brigade of lawyers and investigators from gathering intelligence that was later used against those they considered threats. Congress could have cut the White House budget to stop this abuse, but it did virtually nothing.

After the bombing of the Murrah Federal Building in Oklahoma in 1995, the Clinton administration, the Democrats, and their supporters in the mainstream media worked hard to establish the fiction that the bombing was the work of fringe elements of the Vast Right-Wing Conspiracy. New evidence is emerging that suggests there might be some connection to our current terrorist foes. But Clinton and his friends were convinced it was the Right Wing that was responsible.

Thus, new federal laws were passed which gave the FBI and other agencies new tools to investigate domestic terrorists. An entire class of "angry white males" was identified, and gray-haired men wearing flannel shirts and red suspenders and living in western states were deemed to be dangerous and worthy of federal investigative attention.

The fact that there has not been a single important indictment or conviction of any of these supposed large-scale, highly organized angry white male domestic terrorists has somehow escaped the notice of the mainstream media that helped to create this ridiculous bogeyman.

While the FBI was sent out to investigate this *horrible* domestic threat, Osama bin Laden was establishing his deadly terrorist network right under our noses.

The fact that most of these men from the right were patriots, concerned that Bill Clinton and his strident wife, Hillary, were intent on trashing the Constitution and taking away their Second Amendment rights, meant little to FBI agents assigned to investigate them. If agents complained about investigating citizens who worshipped God and adhered to the Constitution, nobody ever heard of it.

FBI agents mostly do what they are told to do.

Which brings me to this: while it's all well and good to build a massive government intelligence structure to defeat foreign terrorists, it is the undeniable truth that *our federal government is still hung up on political correctness and refuses to concentrate on the real terrorists, out of fear of being accused by a vocal few of racial profiling.*

Instead, leaders and bureaucrats take the easiest path to try to defeat our enemies: they treat every citizen as if he or she may be a suspect. In order to do that, they need new laws that give them incredible new powers, *at the expense of our liberties.*

The folks who love government have found common cause. Love of government has no party lines, apparently. Members of the Republican and Democratic parties join hands in favor of a massive buildup of federal agencies, federal intelligence ranks and law enforcement officers. No thought is ever given, apparently, to downscaling a single federal agency, no matter how ridiculous, how expensive or how irrelevant.

Thus, the federal government grows and grows.

After the terrorists are defeated, what remains is a massive intelligence-gathering machine that can be aimed at any group, foreign or domestic, that's considered a threat to national security.

Those currently holding the power apparently learned nothing from the abusive years of the Clinton administration. In the wrong hands, that machine, currently being assembled to fight foreign terrorists, can be misused against the political enemies of a newly elected president.

Those enemies may be traditional ethical dissenters and common political adversaries.

But the former Clinton administration should serve as a reminder that once created, the terrible forces of the federal government *will* be used. We have learned the hard way that there are no real safeguards against political abuse.

True bureaucrats don't know how to act otherwise, and dishonest politicians couldn't care less about your rights. To some in politics, winning is everything. Those who call themselves Republicans or Conservatives should remember that.

Nevertheless, there is a vast coming-together of all those who believe that the federal government is the answer to all our woes. They are from the Hard-Left and from the ranks of the Republicans who call themselves moderates.

I'm certain that supporters of the emerging Green Party are also celebrating. After all, big government is what they need to enforce their extreme environmental agenda.

The new third party is all of those who love government, wallow in government, know of no other way, no other solution and, not incidentally, have no other employment.

The new third party is made up of bureaucrats and big-government politicians and is supported by dreamers who crave security over all else and can't appreciate the fact that liberty is exactly what sets us apart from all other civilizations.

If we allow the new third party (call them Government-Loving Bureaucrats) to trade our liberty for security, then all we'll have left is real estate. We must not let that happen.

# CHAPTER TWO—
# Hard-Left Hates Whistleblowers

I am not anti-government as some might suggest, but I am an expert witness. I was a federal employee for 30 years, and much of that time I served as a federal agent.

I was alarmed by the stark differences between how the U.S. government postures itself toward an ever-growing number of citizens who insist that agencies be tolerant, friendly, honest, fair, and generous to the population, versus the manner in which so many federal agencies treat honest employees (very poorly).

After nearly 40 years of viewing it from both inside and out, let me state it plainly: When it comes to the treatment of honest employees—some of whom have dedicated their lives in so many ways—as an employer, the federal government is one mean bastard.

Little armies of incompetents, sycophants, suck-ups and go-alongs inhabiting the federal work force are treated better by the managers and directors of the agencies than the honest, ethical employees who see a wrong and then try to right it.

Incompetents are treated better because they keep their mouths shut.

Two recent events have resurfaced this issue for me. First, there was an article in the business section of my local newspaper reporting that while employment opportunities are not as good in the private sector as college graduates would like, jobs are plentiful in the federal government.

That's because so much of the federal workforce is eligible for retirement. Statistics tells us that fully 50 percent of the federal workforce can retire in the next few years.

Second, was the most recent filing of my IRS forms and the realization that it would be sometime in May before the first dollar of my own labors went to me and my family instead of to the government.

I shudder to think about all those young, idealistic, honest college graduates who will have their bubbles burst within days of beginning their careers. What also makes me nervous is that as their honesty and integrity are tested, and they first learn of some of the awful things going on all around them, they'll fail the test. They won't simply walk off the job; they'll make their dirty little deal with their new employer because the benefits are good and because they believe that somehow it will get better.

But without serious attention to this problem, it will only get worse.

Consider that for every whistleblower who goes public, who risks it all then loses everything, there are approximately 50,100 fellow employees who have swallowed hard, walked into their boss' office and made some attempt to give the American taxpayer a better product by addressing a waste, an abuse, some fraud or some incompetence.

And then they're summarily tossed out of their boss' office after being told to shut up, to stop rocking the boat, to grow up, and to stop being a pest, or they'll be very sorry.

For all the hoopla that's given to searching for, and then finding, honest people to work in the federal service, you should be aware that the name given to those who insist on doing things the right way is "Goo Goos." That's the best compliment Washington insiders can think of to describe honest federal employees.

That should give you some idea about how bad it really is.

The result is that many federal employees end up choosing the path that guarantees the least trouble for their careers: silence. Some don't even approach the boss because they've heard about what has happened to others who have tried. Honest employees scolded the first, second or third time by bureaucrats determined to march in place until retirement, eventually get the message.

The whistleblower that simply refuses to get with the program gets both barrels of the angry management scatter-gun for their troubles, and that usually means their career is over.

The otherwise good employee who chooses to remain silent never gets used to a corrupted workplace. Instead, he sulks or complains, and thus, becomes a part of the problem.

Remember though, he *wanted* to be a part of the solution until he learned the cost to his career. He's still working there and would readily adapt to excellence, if leaders get around to reinstating excellence.

Making the transition from being an honest citizen to becoming a dishonest, corrupt government employee is such an institutional problem in the federal system that it even has a name; it's called losing your virginity. Thus, otherwise honest people become part of the massive morale problem that today grips the huge, wasteful federal bureaucracy ever tighter, even if they're only guilty of remaining silent in the face of obvious corruption.

Today, federal government agencies build at least 10 percent into their budgets to cover abuse, theft, incompetence and waste. With a budget in the trillions, that adds up to a lot of your cash.

You would think that there would be a program to encourage honest employees to come forward to stop a gross abuse of the taxpayer's hard-earned money. You would think there would be a South Lawn ceremony at which the president of the United States would thank those who have had the courage to stop a fraud or an incompetent waste of your money.

You would think that in a time of war, there would be no place for laziness, waste, deceitfulness or other forms of employee misconduct. However, if you think that, you would be dead wrong.

What's my proof? Linda Tripp, Billy Dale, and my former FBI partner Dennis Sculimbrene, as well as many others who fell victim to a federal government that moved swiftly to punish them when they became whistleblowers.

What the Clinton administration did to them was so utterly wrong, and yet the new administration has been in place for some time now. Yes, I know there is a war going on, but how difficult would it be for the federal government to right the wrongs committed against these decent whistleblowers by ordering the attorney general to settle their cases immediately so as to end both the financial and professional suffering?

If the Bush administration would simply do that, it would send a strong signal to others inside our government, those who have significant information relevant to the health of our national security, to come forward now and tell us what they know.


## Hypocrite of the Year Award

Is the media now realizing the importance of whistleblowing? The editors of *Time* magazine seem to have suddenly discovered the dangers and benefits that come from whistleblowing. The cover of a recent issue features their "Persons of the Year"—three women who blew the whistle on corporate and government incompetence or wrongdoing.

I don't want to discourage whistleblowers or those who choose to ride on their coattails; surfacing the truth about corporate and government wrongdoing is usually considered a good thing.

But I find it difficult to understand how some can turn truth on and off like a switch.

Not long ago this country went through a wrenching period which ended in a president's impeachment. Not only was Bill Clinton chasing skirts in the Oval Office, but he and his administration were gutting national security safeguards to the point that we—as a nation—were seriously vulnerable to espionage and terrorist attacks.

Now there were those who tried to blow the whistle on Bill Clinton and his administration, but they were attacked repeatedly by the media, including *Time*. After Monica Lewinsky became a worldwide embarrassment to our country, *Time* dutifully reported that there was a Vast Right Wing Conspiracy hell-bent on Clinton's destruction.

They downplayed numerous abuses and said it was all about sex. Somehow, Clinton Haters were only out to get Bill and Hillary.

They actually reported this with graphs and photographs showing how the conspiracy worked. In the *Time* version of events, it was not important that the serious allegations about Clinton were true. What was important was the appearance, the personality, or the political leaning of the whistleblowers. Thus, truth-tellers like Linda Tripp were demonized while the shocking conduct of a president was down played as a lovable rogue's lifestyle preferences.

Lost in the wall of noise about what sex is and what is is, was an obvious misconduct on the part of the President of the United States, including the dismantling of national security safeguards previously mentioned. Apparently to *Time,* there is a time when it's appropriate to talk about national security and a time when it is not appropriate. Could it be that *Time* is more interested in FBI incompetence during a Republican administration, when it's George W. Bush's FBI and not Bill Clinton's FBI?

But consider that if the warnings about national security, beginning in 1993, had been taken seriously and not written off as the rants of the Right Wing, it might have been possible to head off the horrific terrorist attacks in 2001. As early as the summer of 1993, national security professionals were sounding warnings about the Clinton administration's incompetence in protecting this nation. Today, there are few who would argue that, for whatever reason, Bill Clinton dropped the ball on Osama bin Laden.

Despite the efforts of many to get the attention of *Time* and other media, this developing story was ignored. They only seemed interested in joining the White House in the most remarkable smear campaign to ever rain down on those who were simply and courageously trying to warn the nation of a dangerous administration.

Regardless of the reasons for Clinton's incompetence in national security, *Time* had a duty—at *least* insofar as they share the same real estate as the rest of us—to play the story straight.

But instead, they chose to become part of the Clinton spin machine. Is it sufficient to conclude they were just unable to connect the dots? I believe the evidence is so overwhelming on this score that not even Inspector Clouseau could have missed the mountain of clues.

But, when my bestselling book, *Unlimited Access: An FBI Agent Inside the Clinton White House,* was published, *Time* had a field day—along with the rest of the national media—destroying my credibility on the say-so of the Clinton White House. My book was 98 percent about the national security breakdown inside the Clinton White House and 2 percent about the ill manners of some Hard-Left Democrats.

Nevertheless, national media like *Time* scoffed at the well-documented claims of a senior FBI agent who had been working in the Clinton White House, full-time, for more than two years.

They preferred to believe that I had lost my mind. History unfolded, however, and has vindicated me. The lack of DNA evidence for Clinton's reckless womanizing, as described in my book, is hardly mentioned these days. What is recalled is that I was a serious whistleblower who tried to surface wrongdoing, abuse, and corruption occurring in the White House, right under the nose of the national media.

Back then, *Time* thought differently about whistleblowing. They went on to ignore or demonize every single whistleblower that bravely stepped forward to describe Clinton's shameful conduct or Clinton administration corruption.

Most of these whistleblowers were women, like federal investigator Jean Lewis, or Linda Tripp, or Juanita Broaddrick, or Paula Jones, or Kathleen Willey, or Gennifer Flowers. All were attacked and dismissed as bimbos and liars.

*Time* magazine had it wrong: *Clinton* was the liar.

But these courageous women will never grace the cover of *Time* magazine, even if the passage of time has proven them to be correct in their claims. You see, media giants like *Time* are so corrupt that they actually believe they don't need to admit their mistakes.

Slanting or misreporting the news is a serious corruption because it can lead the general public and political leaders on dangerous and time-wasting wild goose chases. The fact that *Time* is politicized or is a one-party magazine is no excuse for lying.

I cannot wait for the first *Time* magazine whistleblower to step out of the pages and tell the truth about how corrupted *Time* is. I look forward to that glorious day.

# Congressional Baby Steps

Senators Grassley and Leahy have introduced legislation entitled the FBI Reform Act of 2002 to ostensibly address systemic problems at the Federal Bureau of Investigation. Everyone seems to agree that some change is necessary, but I have seen little in the Grassley/Leahy bill that gives me confidence that things will improve at the FBI if this law passes and is signed by President Bush.

What's proposed can only be considered baby steps toward a solution to a much bigger problem. Given the numerous and recent well-publicized missteps, the public is ready to believe FBI reforms are necessary. There is a unique opportunity to make meaningful changes. So why won't the Senate propose real reform?

A key element of the proposed reform is to bring FBI employees under a whistleblower umbrella of protection by making them eligible for all the benefits afforded other federal employees currently covered under the existing Whistleblower Protection Act. Sounds promising, huh? But before we consider the merits of the rest of what these well-meaning senators propose, we should first determine how useful the inclusion of FBI employees under this act would be.

Today, there are *no* benefits for federal employees afforded by the current Whistleblower Protection Act. The only benefits fall to federal agencies whose legions of lawyers have managed over the years to totally gut the act. The current protections are as tattered and useful as a blown-out bumbershoot on a cold, windy day in Chicago.

Federal employees who trudge off to work each day believing they have an obligation and a right to surface serious wrongdoing will get the shock of their soon-to-be-ending careers if they ever try to implement this act. There are no protections!

Major whistleblower advocates like The Patrick Henry Center, the Project on Government Oversight (POGO) and the Government Accountability Project (GAP) have been working for years to get some teeth back into the whistleblower laws.

Ironically, the more incompetent and corrupt a federal agency is, the greater the benefits for the guilty federal agency. Seasoned agency managers can pretend they have a whistleblower protection system while unleashing a legal and professional *jihad* against any honest, well-meaning insider who sets out to correct a serious wrong.

Under the existing meaningless law, revengeful bureaucrats will always get away with it!

I'm certainly an advocate of following the chain of command to try to correct serious wrongdoing, especially at a time like this. After all, employee managers are hired to be honest and paid to correct problems.

But there's no evidence that even now, when we are at war and good performance counts for more, anything has gotten better.

Actually, the war provides new excuses for keeping the lid on any internal problems: silencing whistleblowers can be claimed as a good thing to do—*in the interest of national security!*

But consider that two of the terrorists received approvals from the INS for their student visa applications, by ordinary mail, to the flight school in Florida where they learned how to crash airplanes into our buildings, exactly six months after the worst attack on America!

Are there more than a few honest INS insiders yearning to come forward *right now* to make a report to a person in a position of authority—someone who could make positive change—so that incompetence like this can be prevented in the future? Will INS employees come forward? The answer is "Yes"... if they want to end their career in the federal service. It's just that simple.

Those of us who have tried to surface national security shortcomings are well aware of the real reason bureaucrats move to silence a whistleblower. Corrupt, scared, lazy federal managers' motivations often have more to do with covering up inadequate responses to earlier warnings. These cowards don't want to be seen by higher-ups as incompetent, cynical, or uncaring.

Want real whistleblower protections? Want real reform inside the FBI and other important federal agencies? Then strengthen existing whistleblower protection laws and severely punish those bureaucrats who are caught trying to silence our brave whistleblowers.

How about having that awards ceremony on the South Lawn of the White House to celebrate the courage of those honest federal employees who were mad as hell and refused to take it anymore! Our soldiers are fighting overseas to protect our freedom, and we rightfully praise them. Our whistleblowers are fighting to maintain some semblance of excellence here at home. Wouldn't you agree, considering the odds stacked against them, that whistleblowers deserve more than scorn?

Agency bureaucrats often label whistleblowers as crazy, and in the current kill-the-messenger environment, maybe they are. But passing a feel-good bill that does little to protect whistleblowers is not exactly the sanest thing to do—especially during times of war.

# Dangerous U.S. Customs

Parents are worried about terrorism, and what's really scary is what may be parked a couple hundred yards away from their children's public school, according to one courageous whistleblower who had the guts to come forward.

Thousands of pressurized railcars cross U.S. borders daily, and U.S. Customs is doing next to nothing to inspect them, making each one a handy vehicle for contraband distribution. Worse, deadly chemicals, available to any terrorist with phony identification and a credit card, can be purchased in Mexico and parked indefinitely all over the U.S. at thousands of rental rail spurs. Railcars can even be moved back and forth with a laptop computer and placed in key areas for later illegal drug off-loading or worse.

Fill one of these pressure tanks with diesel fuel oil and fertilizer, and what do you have? The world's largest pipe bomb. Imagine: If one Ryder rental truck-bomb in Oklahoma City destroyed half of a giant federal office building, what could a huge rail tanker filled with poison gas or explosives do to your average city?

Are these the concerns of hysterical citizens looking under every bed for a post-September 11, 2001, bogeyman? Hardly. U.S. Customs federal agents have been warning about this danger for years without any real action being taken to stop Customs managers. When several U.S. Customs agents brought their concerns to the local FBI office in California, fearing their own agency had been compromised, nothing happened, they claim. Finally, frustrated by inaction and fear, they went public. Some have testified in front of the U.S. Senate, but still there is no substantive action to address this real danger.

Former U.S. Customs federal agent Darlene Fitzgerald-Catalan contacted my foundation—The Patrick Henry Center—because she heard that I tried to warn others about national security dangers but had also hit a brick-wall when agency bureaucrats simply did not want to listen. She thought we could help.

Darlene is a classic whistleblower. The difference is that Fitzgerald-Catalan and six other federal agent associates, and a U.S. prosecutor, walked out en masse in 1999, but their brave mutiny, complete with staged public protests, netted them nothing but scorn and retribution from U.S. Customs managers.

Fitzgerald-Catalan can cite many examples of agent managers who reeked of incompetence. But, U.S. Customs managers' inability to manage agents and investigations is one thing. When Fitzgerald-Catalan tried to conduct pressurized railcar investigations to determine the extent of contraband coming into the States from a corrupt rail yard in Mexico, her investigations were shut down by worried managers. When other agents attempted to help her, they were punished severely and subjected to endless administrative probes, designed to get them to resign or retire.

Every time a federal agent exhibited interest in conducting a serious probe of railcar smuggling, he or she found themselves on the wrong end of U.S. Customs' fury. They were followed and subjected to false allegations designed to destroy their careers. They even found hidden video surveillance cameras aimed at their personal residences that they believe were meant to be seen so as to intimidate them into leaving the railcar investigation alone.

Did they have grounds to suspect that pressurized cars were being used to haul illegal drugs or even more dangerous materials? Why would anybody pay to have empty cars moved about the United States? Of course nobody would, and that is why the railroad detectives and honest U.S. Customs agents knew something was up! Not only did they find cars filled with illegal drugs, but they had railroad detectives point out numerous cars that even though their weight records showed them to be empty, were actually filled with mysterious material weighing tons.

Why did Fitzgerald-Catalan's managers shut down her investigation and punish anyone who tried to help her or who came to her defense when Customs internal affairs agents set out to ruin her? In an interview in Boston recently, she told me that at first, she believed that Customs managers were just being good old boys and may have been jealous of her high-performance investigations. But when a more sinister pattern of punishment and harassment began, it was obvious to her that more was going on than the mere damage to some lesser investigator's ego.

"Besides," Fitzgerald-Catalan explained, "it didn't matter what the other agents did or didn't do in their jobs. Those deemed to be in favor with management and who went along with the corruption were rewarded with cash incentives and favorable notes in their personnel files. Those who rocked the boat and questioned mysterious decisions by management to back off of certain investigations—like pressurized railroad cars—were rewarded with scorn, punishment and endless internal affairs investigations."

Darlene Fitzgerald-Catalan has written a book, *U.S. Customs: Badge of Dishonor*, describing the incredible events leading up to her voluntary resignation in 1999. At that time, she worried about out of control drug trafficking with pressurized rail cars as the vehicle. Today, Fitzgerald-Catalan is glad she brought her concerns to the public because she and her former U.S. federal agent associates understand the real potential for disaster.

Fitzgerald-Catalan stated, "When a federal agency tasked with the protection of U.S. citizens' interests is too incompetent or too corrupt to do the job, something needs to be done."

## Commerce or Chaos?

You can't make a dollar if everyone is hiding inside their houses, so get out there and buy something! Of course, this is the dilemma facing the U.S. Border Patrol. If they stop and inspect too much traffic, then commercial interests will scream and shout about it.

The primary business of America is business, if recent accounts of resistance by American and Canadian businessmen to enhanced border security is any measure. Human life seems to come in a distant second place. Heaven forbid that any of us receive our gimcracks and gadgets a day or two late because some Teamster driving a truck had to wait in a long line to cross one of our "Mickey Mouse" border checkpoints.

Commerce aside, we would not want to interrupt any plans that your average Middle Easterner has for driving down to Southern California for a nice cozy family reunion. Since we don't profile anybody in the Land of the Politically Correct, lest we offend, there should not be much delay for them. On the way back to Canada (unless he stops to blow up a bus load of people) perhaps our welcome visitor can conduct a video surveillance of a nuclear power plant to pinpoint weaknesses.

Evidence of this U.S. Border Patrol nightmare can be found in the latest Government Accounting Office report that says that our borders are still a sieve, especially the Canadian border. Terrorists can pour across our borders at will, apparently, and the federal government—long before September 11, 2001—knew this. Yet nothing substantial has been done about it. The Canadian border is especially troublesome because of documented evidence of several well-known terrorists who were easily able to establish residence in Canada, then waltz over the border to implement their deadly tricks.

Not to put too fine a point on it, but the terrorists who were thankfully arrested by the FBI before they could light their fuses, were set to blow up the Los Angeles International Airport, New York City's subway system and the Holland Tunnel. Or was it the Lincoln Tunnel? Hey, what's a tunnel or two when you consider the commerce that could have been interrupted by pesky and nosy U.S. Border Patrol agents poking under every canvas cover?

Now I know there are those who are going to say, "Aldrich, don't you ever stop? We have our guy in the White House right now! Become a cheerleader, for Pete's sake!"

Yes, I prefer George W. Bush to Bill Clinton or Al Gore any day of the week. But I have also learned a few things about politics in Washington. The lobbyists, who pound on the heads of every elected official night and day, are not lobbyists for the human race.

They are sent here to make sure the wheels of government turn smoothly. They are here to engage in commerce. They are not security experts, and they clearly don't understand what their incessant pressure is doing to our nation's security. What's more, I'm not sure there's evidence that even if they knew, they would care.

It's people like you and me who are lobbyists for national security and the human race. We don't get paid to do it, and we have no large sums of money to hand out to promote our cause. All we can do is offer good advice based on common sense and experience—not to mention very recent history—to the people we have elected, and hope and pray that they put a higher value on a single human life—especially an American life—when they decide how many new federal agents they will send to patrol the borders.

Sending them *right now* would be a grand idea.

# CHAPTER THREE—
# Hard-Left Theme Park

Nothing brings more joy to the heart of your average Hard-Left Agenda member than the thought that just 90 miles from our shores there exists a Communist paradise that has resisted all the efforts of others to bring freedom and capitalism back to the poor souls who have to live there. I'm speaking, of course, of Cuba.

Consider the nonstop reports of human rights abuses in communist Cuba. Fidel Castro is nothing more than a lying, murderous dictator who has oppressed an island nation for more than 40 years. These facts are indisputable. That a former Hard-Left Democratic president named Carter recently visited Castro to bring good wishes and tribute from the Hard-Left is no surprise.

The Hard-Left has had an affection for Castro's politics since he seized power decades ago.

A focus of this human tragedy is South Florida where thousands of Cuban refugees settled after fleeing their homeland. As a young boy growing up in Hialeah, Florida, I went to school with hundreds of Cuban children whose parents were lucky enough to get out. That's how everyone in south Florida talked about fleeing Cuba—they were fortunate enough to "get out." It truly was a great escape, like something straight out of a World War II P.O.W. movie.

For years, Cubans boarded small boats and made the 90-mile trek from Cuba to Key West, if they were lucky. If they were unlucky and missed the Florida Keys, they often drifted north, getting caught in the currents of the Gulf Stream, never to be seen again.

Sometimes, as in the case of Elian Gonzales, the passengers on the crowded boats were found by south Florida fishermen out for a day of sun and fun. But all too often, the boats' passengers fell victim to the fierce storms that raged in the Atlantic. Thousands died fleeing Castro.

But why did they flee? What were they trying to get away from? What were they seeking? What did they hope to find in America?

Many have reduced these brave Cuban patriots' desires and the risks they took to the material. That's because so many see life in America as a continual quest for more things. The dignity and wonder of life is too often defined by the number of items stocked on our grocery shelves and our ability to purchase as many goods as we can carry off in our new luxury SUVs.

To be fair, more than a few Cuban refugees have been reduced to tears as they walked through our giant superstores for the very first time, gazing at the great quantities of food and overwhelming variety that we take for granted. In their homeland everything is rationed, including basics like toilet paper, sugar, coffee and other staples.

Seeing their joy, their excitement, we easily mistake their emotions as evidence that the differences between living in Cuba and living in America are all about the kind of car one drives or the number of chickens one can put into the family pot each week. How wrong we are if we think that.

In 1982, I was smuggled into the hotel room of an old Cuban woman visiting the U.S. for a few precious weeks. She was the grandmother of a very good friend of mine. Most Cubans view the FBI much like we, as Americans, view the KGB. Castro had preached for years about alleged FBI and CIA plots that were underway to undermine his power-base. But, she wanted to talk to me, an FBI agent, because she wanted to tell as many people as possible about the horrible fear she lived with day in and day out.

Was this brave woman afraid of terrorists or criminals or wild animals? No, she was simply afraid of Fidel Castro and the thousands of Castro agents that had been recruited all over the island of

Cuba. And, what purpose did these block captains have? Why did Castro want an agent on every single block in every single town on the island? To spy and report suspicious activities, of course! Every citizen on the island of Cuba is being watched around the clock by Castro's agents. When a Castro agent suspects dissident activity on the part of anyone, no matter how young or old, odds are, the truck with the troops will arrive at night and that citizen will disappear for awhile, or maybe forever.

This is the constant fear that the Cuban people live with. In seeking a meeting with an FBI agent, this brave old woman was risking imprisonment. South Florida was riddled with Castro agents on the lookout for any signs of dissent. Not only would she be in serious trouble, but her relatives would be also. Castro has a way of being especially angry with those whom he considers disloyal.

Was this grandmother trying to tell me she wanted more coffee or bread? Was she risking so much to send a message to America that her nation needed more medicine or panty hose?

The courage she displayed that day was the same courage displayed by the thousands of Cubans who had come before her. They were trying to tell us—we, the people who they believed to be their friends and supporters—that they had lost their liberty and their freedoms to an angry and evil dictator who had instituted in their land the most oppressive form of government.

The fact that they don't enjoy a steady supply of coffee, or bread or toilet paper is the result of a loss of liberty, stolen by a treacherous and murderous form of government, and not because the United States supports an embargo designed to drive Castro out.

But Jimmy Carter and his ilk will never understand that. They believe that one day some Communist leader will get it right and communism will prevail so that we can all reach that one-world Utopia envisioned and lusted after by the Hard-Left. The American Hard-Left had high hopes that Castro could pull it off. The fact that he has failed and his people still suffer so much has not diminished the American Hard-Left's affection for him, as evidenced by the smiling face of Jimmy Carter as he embraced a murderous dictator.

The Elian Gonzalez case is a reminder of just how fond the Hard-Left is of Castro and Cuba. So determined was Bill Clinton to normalize relations with Fidel that he promised to send young Elian back so he could not be used as an embarrassment to Castro's failed communist experiment.

The exercise backfired on Clinton, however, as good citizens of this nation rose up in significant protest. Many say that the Elian Gonzalez case was one of the deciding factors in the minds of Floridians as they went to the polls to decide their next president.

## *Fathers Have Rights in Cuba?*

In all the scuffle about Elian, there emerged an interesting debate about father's rights. I found it ironic that those on the Hard-Left who have worked for so long to demonize men, would suddenly circle around and support Elian's father, a self-described devoted Communist.

The fact is, for 30 years or more, the rights of American fathers have been steadily eroded. From no-say in abortions, to no-say in divorce, to no-say in custody, to no-say in child support or how it's spent, to no-say in visitation, to no-say in day care issues, the feminists of the Hard-Left have slowly, but surely, emasculated men.

But magically, in the case of Cuban-born Elian, having a father around is absolutely necessary!

For nearly three generations, fathers—indeed all men, (and those who could speak for them, such as the few women who seem to actually like men and still possess some common sense)—have stood very, very silent while their rights have been eroded out of existence.

Inexplicably, American men seem docile as puppies when it comes to their rights. Scratch their bellies and you own them, or so it appears.

Today's American male, poor sad shell of a man that he's become, has all the rights of a beast of burden, bred for working and ripe for doses of verbal whipping when caught misbehaving by the "she-males".

The only right today's American male has is to be accused and abused.

Thanks to the Hard-Left, American men have become mostly

irrelevant in a child's life. Forty percent of children are born out of wedlock. Men? Who needs them? The children who aren't aborted and do have married parents have a 50 percent chance of becoming a child of divorce.

Millions of men's other children are murdered in the womb—but men are prohibited from stopping it, no matter how much they would love and support those unborn children. Men have no say, according to feminists.

How many of the divorces were caused by the strident, petulant nagging of a feminist-leaning woman, raised and educated by our society to believe that today's man is worse than something she'll step on as she makes her way to the next power-lunch?

How many of these no-fault divorces were initiated by the woman?

How many children cry for their missing daddies just because these women want to be fulfilled?

Lately, no one seems able to make a convincing case that one American man—one American father—matters a whit anymore in the raising of a single American child, girl or boy. This tells you how deep the damage is: only the size of a man's wallet is seen as the issue these days.

Suddenly, out of nowhere, comes an enormous wave of public opinion that Elian's dad is important, and a son and his dad need to be together, no matter what! Even if Elian has to live in a slave state, which does not seem to matter. Somehow the wishes of the mother who drowned to give her young son a chance at liberty and *freedom*, mean nothing against a man's—a father's—rights!

It's a miracle! A grand awakening to the importance of fatherhood and the relevance of American men in their own children's lives? A renewed respect for the loyal, dedicated labors of the typical American male? A recognition of the average American man's pride in supporting and defending his family, his wife, and yes, his children?

Not so fast! This was not about American men's rights! This had nothing to do with American dads—unless you count their fantasies about the way they wished things were.

This was about a Cuban Communist's perceived rights. So it's OK, since a Cuban man doesn't have any rights. Mr. Gonzalez lives in a police state, and the state owns the child.

# *The Hard-Left Ignores All the Facts*

The Elian Gonzalez case served to remind us just how deep the love goes between America's Hard-Left and Cuba's murderous communist dictator, Fidel Castro. The matter of a father's rights was just a theme used by the Hard-Left to offer up a sacrifice to one of their most celebrated heroes.

The Bush administration has an opportunity to address communism in our hemisphere as they begin to investigate how Castro and Cuba have provided safe-haven and training for worldwide terrorism. Until Bush can get around to that, citizens of Cuba will remain prisoners, and continue to live in poverty and terror.

How the Hard-Left can point to Cuba as one of their success stories defies logic and strains credulity. But, being wrong has never impeded the progress of the Hard-Left. They continue to gaze south and imagine warm breezes, equality, full bellies, and universal health care for all—all who are members of the Communist Party, that is. Let the rest eat cake.

# CHAPTER FOUR—
# Hard-Left's Big Entertainment

Big entertainment is a combination of what Hollywood-types churn out plus what used to be called news. The mainstream media no longer attempts to report the news. For years they have been engaged in "making" the news and supporting whatever issues the Hard-Left is interested in promoting.

How else do you explain the contrived hysteria over Enron? When I was an FBI agent I worked on white-collar crime investigations. My background and education is in accounting, so I worked closely with bank officials, corporate executives, CPAs, accountants, auditors, and others engaged in the science of accounting.

It was not long before my growing experience caused the FBI management to assign me major cases. The *major* of a white-collar crime case is partly determined by the number of people involved and their positions in the company, but mostly, the *major* is determined by the dollar amount of the loss.

The FBI has a dollar-threshold that must be met before the agency will agree to handle a case.

In each case we prosecuted, one common thread existed: greed. The most important thing you should know about Enron is that in white-collar crimes, including Enron, there is nothing new under the sun, even though the mainstream media would try to make you believe otherwise.

Businesses come and go and some fail in a rather spectacular way. However, nothing we see today can possibly match the crash of those dot-com companies whose collapses began in the year 2000. Review the statistics: there are thousands and thousands of people who are out of jobs and are financially broke because of all those business failures. Yes, the media did focus on some of that, but never to the degree that they are focusing on Enron.

Ask any employee who worked at any of the high-tech companies what happened when the company gave them stock as employee bonuses. More than a few of those stocks could not be traded due to a corporate practice called handcuffing. Employees could own the stock, but for long periods of time they could not convert or sell the stock.

I have a close relative who was given large blocks of stock—as employee benefits—in a well known high-tech company, but he could not convert the stocks to cash, nor could he trade it. We were so happy for his success, and at one Christmas gathering we joked about being in the presence of a millionaire. His family seemed set for life, and his children could plan to attend the college of their choice. He and his wife would be secure, forever—as soon as they could sell the stock.

Today, they are lucky to be considered hundred-aires, and he's fortunate to have his job. But what of his plans for the future, which were destroyed? What makes him different from any of the Enron employees who lost everything because they had a portion of their savings wrapped up in 401(k) plans that were also handcuffed?

My relative's company is still doing business, but the stock went from a high near ninety dollars, to a low of five, and it's still dropping.

Does the slow death of this major company mean the media is not interested in finding out how much the corporate barons there collected before the bottom fell out? And, what about the salaries of those greedy corporate executives? Could there be a memo or two warning that some manner of business tactic was contributing to the overall demise of the company? You can bet your life that there were thousands of cover-your-assets style memorandums written for that very reason—so that the writers could cover their rear-ends in a situation where the end was obviously near.

Using a memo for this purpose is as old as the abacus—but that does not make one a whistleblower.

I'll bet if we look, we will see major cash contributions from my relative's corporation to politicians on the Left side of the political aisle. Would that make the story newsworthy? Will that get them investigated by the FBI? Don't hold your breath

No, national attention only comes if the mainstream media is fed the notion that somehow a very successful current administration could be hit by the embarrassing disclosures. In the case of my close relative, his particular company is not known for its heavy support of Conservatives, but they *do* support the Hard-Left agenda.

I guess the mainstream media will not be interested in knowing what happened to my close relative and how his financial future has been destroyed by corporate greed.

## *Is There a Vast Left Wing Conspiracy?*

I attended a dinner in 2002 that turned out to be a gathering of the Vast Right Wing Conspiracy.

I didn't know I was going to be with this controversial group until the emcee announced that's who we really are. Of course, Cal Thomas was kidding. But, I was reminded of who Hillary thought we were and how such a label marginalized us.

I came to this event looking forward to an evening of solid evidence that there is indeed a Vast *Left* Wing Conspiracy. These like-minded zealots are enabled, in large part, by a biased mainstream media characterized by dishonesty and intolerance for the political views of others.

I dined and laughed with nearly a thousand nicely dressed, polite and honest over-achievers who came at the invitation of Brent Bozell. We were at his Media Research Center's "Dishonors Awards" where we would "Roast the Most Outrageously Biased Liberal Reporters of the Year!"

Video clip after video clip was played to the appreciative audience. Every goofy Hard-Left Liberal's biased blooper proved that Bernard Goldberg was right-on in his book, *Bias*. Most don't need Mr. Goldberg to tell them the media is biased, but I'm glad he's out there for the moderates who have a hard time deciding anything, in spite of all the evidence.

CBS's Dan Rather won top honors for declaring that "A man could lie about any number of things and still be considered honest." Rather made this comment in 2001 after Bill O'Reilly asked him how he could seriously consider Bill Clinton to be an honest man.

In his taped conversation, Rather admitted that he himself lied from time to time—apparently whenever it suited him. How is anybody supposed to know when Rather is lying or when he's telling the truth? Remember that CBS allows him to do this.

It doesn't really matter. The majority of Americans who remain well informed know they cannot trust the usual flacks sent out to defend and support dishonest Hard-Left Liberals. Speaking of flacks, recently John McCaslin, my favorite *Washington Times* reporter, revealed that George Stephanopoulos's memoir, *All Too Human,* was last seen on bookstores' remainder tables, selling for $1. Apparently there are plenty of them at this price. Hurry down.

One of my children brought McCaslin's piece to my attention because they witnessed that day in 1996 when Stephanopoulos called their daddy a "pathological liar" on network TV. He got away with that and now earns seven figures on ABC as a journalist pretending news.

My book has never appeared on any remainder table, and never will. Why? Because truth is still a bestseller.

But for some, truth is not enough. There are millions of moderates who sit on the fence and say they would embrace Conservatives and truth if only we didn't appear so extreme. We're not extreme; we're normal. And polls show the majority of Americans agree with our view.

For my money, an extremist would be somebody who remained undecided, even in the face of overwhelming evidence that Hard-Left Liberals are dishonest and embrace a bankrupt political ideology. It is not in dispute that they are also power hungry, morally corrupt, and unethical when it comes to government and business.

Can so-called moderates be considered the real extremists in the face of irrefutable evidence that more liberalism is wrong, wrong, and wrong for this country? To remain undecided in the face of all the evidence is, at least, a case of extreme denial.

A few great organizations like the Media Research Center watch the mainstream media very closely for daily evidence of real dishonesty. The pile of video and audio evidence just grows and grows.

So, look at the track record of the Hard-Left and then weigh what they have brought us. Then, look at the track record of the Conservatives.

For example, who's always cutting the Pentagon's budget? The Hard-Left!

Who tolerates, even celebrates, the meanest, grossest, crudest depiction of human behavior on TV? Name a shock-jock that isn't a Hard-Left Liberal. Baby Boomer Liberals, old enough to know better, still think bathroom humor is cool. Hard-Left Liberals are forever obsessed with sex, which may indicate—at least to a thinking person—the true depth of a Hard-Left Liberal's immaturity.

And, what group wants to legalize drugs, kill more babies, "inform" our children about homosexuals, open the borders, coddle criminals, and disarm honest taxpayers who simply want the right to defend themselves?

Who wants to take more of your money to pay for all of this silly garbage?

Who promotes the notion of cultural diversity without a scintilla of evidence that there is a better place on the face of the globe in which to live than the United States?

Who's raising a fuss right now over the civil rights of the Taliban prisoners currently held in Cuba? And speaking of Cuba, who promotes normalized diplomatic relations with Castro's police state, an island prison where citizens are treated like cattle and worse?

What political group had eight years of warnings that a very serious terrorist attack was headed our way and had the power to stop it, but did not?

Who continually fans the flames of racial and class hatred? Who takes splinter groups of people, like animal rights advocates, and elevates them into media-created powerhouses by giving them unlimited airtime, simply because they lean Left?

And who, at the very same time, totally ignores the millions of productive citizens who have more important concerns on their minds, like raising a family? Who sneers at women who choose to stay at home and raise their own children? Who constantly degrades men and fathers and trivializes them as so many "Leave It To Beaver" and "Father Knows Best" morons?

The answer to all of the above questions is: Hard-Left Liberals!

Citizens of this great country owe Brent Bozell and his wonderful staff at the Media Research Center a debt of gratitude. Of course they catch Hard-Left Liberals in constant lies—that's like shooting fish in a barrel. But, they get extra credit for doing the ugly business of watching and listening to the *real* pathological liars—those dishonest, narcissistic bores who get paid millions of dollars to create and repeat the outrageous lies used to nurture and protect their Vast Left Wing Conspiracy.


## Hard-Left Punching Bag

Even though our country is engaged in a war that will eventually allow us sleep without the fear of waking up to another September 11, 2001, the Hard-Left finds time to celebrate and remind us of the downfall of Richard M. Nixon.

Watergate happened 30 years ago, but it still causes Hard-Left hearts to flutter!

Ironically, during the most recent anniversary remembrance of this infamous ordeal, an important puzzle-piece of the Clinton administration was firmly set in place. But, the mainstream media found nothing remarkable about a Government Accounting Office report that concluded the Clinton administration was peppered with slobs, vandals, thieves, and crude-acting poor sports who refused to graciously concede victory to President George W. Bush.

Two better examples of how difficult it is to obtain and report truth in Washington do not exist. In the case of Nixon, while it is true that he engaged in conduct that would be considered abusive and reprehensible when judged against the backdrop of the high office he held, from all indications, Nixon was a family man who was faithful and attentive to his family. There are no bimbos to talk about when Nixon's name comes up.

Moreover, nobody could ever say that Nixon's administration was bent on a systematic destruction of national security protections in the White House and the entire Executive Branch. Looking back on the Nixon White House, one could only conclude that national security was a cornerstone of Nixon's overall policy. Even so, Nixon's foreign policy included opening trade and diplomatic doors with Communist China—no small accomplishment.

Critics of Nixon, and of Republicans in general, cannot point a finger at either, relative to the war in Vietnam. Jack Kennedy got us into it, and Lyndon Johnson committed hundreds of thousands of our boys to fight there. When it was all over, more than 58,000 had died in Vietnam, and those soldiers who did come home alive were treated with scorn by the Hard-Left who believe fighting their brother and sister Communists was, and always will be, a sin.

Nixon's ending of the war and the controversial draft began the healing, but he gets no real credit for that.

There are many more accomplishments that Nixon fans can claim, but the point is, he is not as bad as the mainstream media would like you to believe. Yes, there was a third-rate burglary at the Watergate Hotel by clumsy political operatives, and yes, there was an even clumsier attempt to cover it up. Nixon's men had made a colossal mess, but the error was compounded when, out of loyalty, he tried to help them cover up their blunder.

Recall that as a nation we were shocked to hear, on those infamous tapes, a president use such locker room banter. Some even claim that Nixon's swearing did as much to hasten his departure than the actual burglary and cover-up. Americans were convinced at last that Nixon was a man of low moral character, and those who had defended him against a relentless drive by the mainstream media to oust him, finally threw in the towel.

Consider what you might hear if Bill Clinton had taped all of his activities in the Oval Office. If we could play those Clinton tapes, would anyone still think Nixon was evil?

When reporters from the *Washington Post* discovered Watergate they were celebrated as finders of truth. It was about character and sleaze, they said. Their information showed that Nixon was punishing his political enemies, they lectured. It was so very important that Nixon be targeted for impeachment, they intoned. And, since it appeared that a democratic-controlled House and Senate would do just that—with public disapproval of Nixon fanned by a scolding, judgmental media— Nixon finally resigned.

Nixon had been swept into a second term by a landslide victory, but the erosion of public support caused by the laser beam intensity of a ferocious mainstream media was more than anybody could withstand.

So Nixon left office, and his resignation has given the Hard-Left the bogeyman they can trot out each year to amplify grievances they have with the Right.

Since the Hard-Left owns most of the microphones, cameras and newspapers, there isn't much that can be done about this. But there are a few things we *can* do.

For example, when we catch the mainstream media in lies and half-truths, our side could call them on it. There are but a few organizations—Media Research Center and Accuracy In Media—who document these lies well. The trouble is, our guys don't take advantage of them!

This may sound self-serving, and if it is, I apologize, but the GAO report was, in essence, an exoneration of the claims in my book, *Unlimited Access*. When my book was introduced, most of the attacks against me were in the areas of conduct. Condoms on a Christmas tree? Preposterous! Sloppy, arrogant, thieving Clinton staff members grossly unappreciative of and irreverent towards the environment in which they were privileged to work? Unbelievable lies made up by a former FBI Agent in league with the forces of Big Tobacco, the Hard-Left screamed!

The cacophony created by the mainstream media was used to discredit both me and my book, and caused long-lasting damage to my reputation. No matter how much of my book has been proven to be truthful—and I contend the percentage is somewhere near 99 percent and counting—the *Washington Post* still treats me like I'm a crank.

There are no invitations to appear on CBS, a network that has treated me with hostility from day one, and invitations to share what I know about the dysfunctional Clinton White House, or even the beleaguered FBI, are rare from any in the so-called mainstream media. They will never allow me to rehabilitate my credibility and reputation with their audiences because if they did that, they would hurt the Hard-Left, and they would have to admit that they were wrong.

It might be helpful to me, and to those who will come after me, if some on our side would point out my case once in a while to their counterparts on the other side of the aisle.

As long as Conservatives allow the Hard-Left to get away with spreading lies and half-truths about those who come forward to tell the truth, we will have fewer individuals willing to take that risk.

Compare Nixon with Clinton, and then decide for yourself if one or both were lovable rogues or criminal sociopaths. In a "contest" between Nixon and Clinton to determine who was the most corrupt and twisted, the winner has to be Clinton, hands down!

But not if you ask those who labor in Big Entertainment; then you get a different answer.

## *Greed Can Be Good*

Arguments about how biased the mainstream media is may be ended by good old-fashioned greed. If greed triumphs, more than a few news anchors, for whom Conservatives reserve special contempt, will be shown the door. They'll be replaced by new faces waiting in the wings, hair fluffed and short skirts immodestly hiked—but these new arrivals will be there only because they have a lot more to do with entertainment than serious news. And that can only be good news for Conservatives.

ABC News appears to be in meltdown as the bean counters look at the advertising dollars and find that fewer and fewer people are watching what the networks describe as news. First to be brought to the chop block was Ted Koppel. There has apparently been discussion about replacing his late-night news show with David Letterman, who seems unhappy in his current gig. In a nutshell, ABC would lose what they call a serious news program and would gain a show that's billed as pure entertainment, sure to attract the sleepless and lonely.

Those who still want to get news will have to go to Fox News Channel, talk radio or Internet news web sites like NewsMax.com, WorldNetDaily.com and DrudgeReport.com.

That, of course, can only be a good thing for Conservatives who champion the truth.

Just how relevant and cutting-edge has Ted Koppel been, anyway? I once had a chance to test him on this question. At a televised meeting with Conservatives in Washington, D.C., I asked Koppel why he had never invited me on his late-night show to talk about my book, *Unlimited Access*. He stated that my book was old news and no longer relevant. Of course, this was after the election of Bill Clinton to a second term, but before the exposure of the Monica Lewinsky scandal by our friend Linda Tripp.

Here are just two of the themes in the book that I knew were extremely relevant?

First, the Clinton White House Intern program was out of control (and so were the interns), and second, Bill Clinton had continued to be a reckless womanizer and was driving his Secret Service agents crazy. Both stories had been pooh-poohed, suppressed and ignored by the mainstream media. The Ted Koppels of the network news ignored numerous accurate allegations.

Turning to ABC's Sunday morning show, *This Week*, as a paragon of truth and virtue, none other than George Stephanopoulos has taken over. He's supposed to appeal to a younger crowd, except today's younger crowd thinks such shows are old fashioned. They get their news from the Internet.

Stephanopoulos has admitted that he spent the better part of six years getting a notorious liar elected to the White House, then lying to the American public about what was going on inside the Clinton White House. Might I suggest a new name for David Brinkley's creation? How about *Sunday Mornings with Georgie*?

Pretty young women, with no other apparent purpose than to be receptacles for Bill Clinton's excesses, wore a rut in Georgie's carpet on the way to and from intimate liaisons with Bill in the Oval Office, but this traffic never registered on Stephanopoulos's radar screen, in spite of how sharp everyone says he is.

He should be a swell addition to the growing ranks of clueless, but sexy, millionaire news anchors who put ribbons on pigs and then call them pretty.

The demise of *This Week* will bring smiles to those working over at Fox News Channel, the station of choice for those who still insist that news be "fair and balanced."

The question is, where do people go when they want real news but cannot find it in the usual places? The obvious answer is alternative places like talk radio and the Internet, whose forums and audiences are growing in size and credibility every day as it becomes clearer that television is entertainment, but not much else. (Fox News Channel stands as one of the rare exceptions.)

Whoever claimed TV was going to educate the world and make it a better place was either one of the biggest morons ever born, or one of the best liars who ever lived.

## Domestic Enemies of Liberty

> The battle is not to the strong alone; it is to the vigilant, the active, the brave.                                         —Patrick Henry

Since September 11, 2001, the foreign enemies of liberty have been kept at bay.

I believe it's an appropriate time to thank those who have renewed their promise to keep us safe and have delivered on that promise: our military, our FBI agents, our police officers, our firemen, our doctors and nurses. These are the true American heroes of our time.

No catastrophic act of terrorism has occurred within our borders since September 11, which proves that the federal government—under new management—has the ability to fend off our foreign enemies.

Sadly, the domestic enemies of liberty, our homegrown anti-patriots, have been working harder than usual. The Hard-Left behaves like mindless termites, eating away at the foundation of our great nation.

Democrats in the U.S. Senate are monkey-wrenching efforts of the Bush administration to fill the many federal court vacancies that our Supreme Court justices have rightfully labeled a crisis.

As a direct result of these forced vacancies, the 9th Circuit Court of Appeals in California asked a retired judge to return to the bench to help reduce the heavy backlog. His "help" came just days before our precious Independence Day in the form of an appalling and absurd ruling: people could no longer use the phrase "under God" when reciting the Pledge of Allegiance.

Think for a moment about the depth of hatred this man must have for those of us who believe in God.

We see signs of other anti-patriots across the nation. In other forums, like our mainstream media, the Liberals are determined to hold
on to power despite the fact that they are destroying the very foundations upon which this nation stands.

For years The Patrick Henry Center and other like-minded
groups have been reporting that the media is heavily biased against
Conservatives, rarely giving them a voice or an opportunity to state
an opinion.

Meanwhile, outrageous Hard-Left opinions are relentlessly splayed
across newspapers and on television networks. Liberals wage a tireless
war against the Bush administration, slinging mud at our president and
his dedicated team. I'm convinced they won't stop as long as they draw
breath!

You may be aware that a book has been published that describes
in great detail how the Liberal media attempts to silence and shut
out people like us. Author Ann Coulter's *Slander: Liberal Lies About
the American Right,* achieved the #1 spot on the *New York Times* best
seller list—and you know Hard-Left Liberals are stomping mad
about this!

Her book is an excellent and accurate analysis of the prevalent lies in
the mainstream media. She provides many credible examples from Conservatives across the nation, including a reference to my own experiences:

> In light of events since the release of Aldrich's book,
> leading to Clinton's impeachment, contempt citation, and
> disbarment, Aldrich appears to have been vindicated with
> a whoop!

I am, of course, pleased that my account has been corroborated, but,
as Coulter clearly shows, media bias remains rampant. Vindication does
not mean we can lay down our swords of liberty. Rather, the 9th Circuit
Court ruling is a grim reminder to us all of the need to increase our efforts in this battle against the politically correct.

Right now, every conservative voice must be heard!

It is our duty as citizens to be aware of, and active in, the dealings of
our government. Heed Patrick Henry's call to action when he implores,
"Guard with jealous attention the public liberty. Suspect everyone who
approaches that jewel."

It is only with this vigilance and care that we will protect our precious freedoms and fight for the rights, liberties and time-honored traditions handed down from Patrick Henry and our other Founding Fathers.

# CHAPTER FIVE—
# Hard-Left's Nanny State

The Bush administration has an understandable dilemma: they need to protect our nation by making the federal government stronger, while avoiding the creation of a huge federal government machine that the Hard-Left could use after Bush to roll over political opposition.

Imagine a huge federal government machine that Hillary Clinton, as one example, could use if she were to be elected president in 2008. Hillary is so Hard-Left it would be difficult to decide if our biggest threat was from outside our borders, or from our own federal government in a Hillary(!) administration.

## *Consider the Nanny State*

I'm driving an SUV. It's a great truck with cushioned seats, a CD player, cruise control and all-climate air conditioning—but it's still a truck. I used to drive a European sports sedan, but my teenage son was starting to drive, and the speedometer implied that he could go 140 miles per hour if nobody was watching—so the truck seemed like a better choice.

It's a guy color—gunmetal grey. My son and I drive around in our Chevy Tahoe feeling very manly. It has a big cargo area where we store our skill saw and tool chest. My boy managed to find room back there for his 12 inch woofers, explaining that these speakers were necessary if he was expected to drive it.

Imagine my embarrassment when Chevrolet sent a recall notice the other day warning that if I wasn't careful when folding down the back seats, I might pinch my pinky finger! The notice told me that while loading 2x4s or heavy plywood into the back, there was a chance that I, or some innocent loved one, could pinch a finger.

Now, this could be just good public relations on the part of the manufacturer but I don't think so. I smell the federal government in this decision to recall trucks for pinched pinkies. Imagine millions of owners inconvenienced by having to take their trucks to the dealer so that a small plastic cover could be installed to help prevent pinching.

Imagine the cost to the manufacturer, who will now, of course, pass that cost right along to the buyers—but we'll all *feel* better!

I wondered, did anybody at Chevrolet ever have a kid whose finger got pinched by a car door? Now, that's a pinch! Why doesn't Chevy recall every vehicle and install some sort of device to save us from that? And those dangerous 12-volt utility plugs they install everywhere—what about those? How many kids (and dumb adults) have stuck their finger into those outlets to see if there's anything going on in there? Surely the manufacturer can be forced to produce little plastic covers to go over these outlets before somebody gets shocked!

Why is this happening to me—to us? I'll tell you why—there are too many federal government agencies with nothing to do and too much time on their hands. They look for issues to inject themselves into, and they do! I'm willing to bet that some nosy, overbearing control-freak federal bureaucrat heard of a pinky-pinching and saw this horrible trauma as his or her ticket to bureaucracy stardom. After all, it's not sufficient to just show up at these warehouses of make-work federal agencies—no, in order to get ahead you have to champion an issue!

So, minor matters that nobody cares about suddenly can become multi-million dollar crusades with the cost to the general public higher than anybody can possibly calculate.

My son is a vintage sports car buff. He knows about MGs and four-cylinder Porsches with four cams, and Lotus racers with Formula One tubular frames. We were looking at a few of these cars at a recent vintage car race. He asked, "Dad, why do some of these cars have those neat wire wheels with the knock-off hubs, and others have one large nut?"

I should explain to some of our less car-interested readers that these knock-off nuts had little wings, the sole purpose of which was to provide a surface for a manly brass hammer to whack.

In other words, you whacked the wheel off, and then after putting the new wheel on, you whacked the nut in the opposite direction to keep the wheel on. It was very manly, you see, and far more efficient than taking off five or six individual nuts. In a car race, every second counts.

When the wing nuts were outlawed by the U.S. Congress back in the Sixties, it forced car manufacturers to create boring wingless nuts that needed an ugly-looking wrench to get the wheel on and off. All the romance was taken away. The laws were so intrusive that some car manufacturers went right out of business, but who could deny the beauty of a 1967 Austin Healy 3000 with chrome wire wheels and those wonderful chrome wing nuts sparkling in the sunlight? And it was so beautifully loud! Every car enthusiast knows what I'm talking about.

How did this awful tragedy happen? Simple. The maternalistic types like Ralph Nader had been watching too many Hollywood movies. *Ben Hur,* featuring one of our greatest stars, Charlton Heston, had a great chariot race, and one of the chariots had these huge wheel wing nuts that had been made into deadly blades. The bad guy could get up next to our hero and use the deadly spinners to destroy his wheels, but that's not all!

If the chariot went out of control and slammed into a crowd, not only would innocent bystanders get trampled by horses, but they would be cut to ribbons by those deadly spinning blades! Imagine that! Of course, that's all it was—imaginary.

But in the mind of a Ralph Nader, those little wing nuts on the wheels of those dangerous sports cars were worrisome. So, the wing nuts had to go, along with the wooden dashboards and the aircraft-style toggle switches. All sharp edges were softened. Next came seat belts and cushioned surfaces and bumpers that were so high they made the cars look like an old man with his pants pulled up too high. They all but destroyed the European sports car market with their nanny-like concerns.

But, what an improvement! Now we have tiny, ridiculous-looking jellybean vehicles that are boring, but they sure save a lot of gas.

No longer can you get sliced by spinning wheels—but if you're hit by a traditional-sized vehicle, you'll be smashed like a bug in a paper cup.

If Ralph Nader and his ilk feel better, remember, that's all that really counts: feelings.

And that's why my son and I drive a truck—I mean an SUV. It not only makes us feel safer—it is safer! But please, "Mommy," let us enjoy our driving experience. It's one of the few freedoms left to us. Isn't it OK if I want to ignore those pinky-pinching dangers that now face us on a daily basis?

Those "mommies" who drive us crazy with their worries about all other walks of life are now coming after our trucks! What's next?

How about outlawing overbearing, personnel-swamped, maternalistic federal agencies instead?

# Road Trip!

As I drove through various Virginia counties this past summer, picking up and dropping off my children at summer camp, I was amazed to find that in some places gas prices had slipped to $1.40 a gallon for unleaded fuel. A friend called earlier and told me that in Georgia, a gallon costs only $1.15. The other day, while I was visiting a friend's boat, I found that high-test gas had dropped a whopping 20 cents per gallon, as compared to last month.

What ever happened to the dire predications of $3.00 a gallon by the summer of 2001?

Yes, gas prices went up after the start of our War on Terrorism. But gas prices always go up during these times.

Did you ever wonder where hysterical hand-wringers go after gas prices go down? At the peak of the most recent hysteria, some federal government officials agreed to revisit the issue of gas-guzzling SUVs—see how easy it is to get the federal government to react?

The Hard-Left knows that all you have to do is become emotional, hysterical and ignore the facts. Washington will capitulate because it always does.

I've noticed, as I drive along in our SUV, that the politically correct cars are in abundance these days. I notice them because I fear for the safety of the drivers and passengers of what I refer to as jellybean cars. I will confess that I had a small sports coupe at one time, but the no-fear attitude that seems to come with the ownership of those cars was left in the dust of my youth.

Today I can't imagine having an accident in one of those death traps. The fact is, if you insist on driving a tiny car, whether you crash into a tree, an SUV, or into another jellybean car, you're going to be injured, at the very least! Most people are aware that consumer reports say those who drive economy-size vehicles are at risk.

I guess it just goes to show you that members of the Green movement care more about your use of fossil fuels than your life or the safety of your children. They insist car manufacturers make those poorly constructed, weakly protected vehicles due to their belief that these economy cars will yield positive impact on the environment.

Maybe they will, if you don't count the deaths and injuries that result. I guess they figure we have more humans than we know what to do with. We don't have enough whales and baby seals, though, right? If you ask me, their priorities are all mixed up.

There is no question that low-income folks are drawn to these economy-priced cars, but it is often out of necessity. Personally, I would never allow a loved one of mine to purchase a car that is equivalent to an eggshell on wheels. I believe it is a disservice to everyone if we allow the poorly informed to think they are safe behind the wheel of a jellybean car. We are responsible to tell them the truth! Having wheels and tin foil doors does not make it a car!

Another point that comes to mind when writing about cars is the recent legislation passed in New York. Banning the use of cell phones in cars was not only passed by New York legislators, but it is also being considered by other states. I believe there are people out there who cannot multi-task, therefore, they should not use cell phones when they drive.

I was talking to a friend who is highly in favor of outlawing the use of cell phones in cars. I pointed out that it was not the phone itself, but the dialing and conversations that were responsible for the wrecks. She was not to be dissuaded because she made her stand based on her emotions.

The fact that she drives an economy-sized vehicle proves this point all the more. Her fear is that an SUV with a cell phone will end up flattening her like a pancake. The fear this woman has of SUVs and multi-taskers, sets demands that interfere with, and possibly even cripple, progress made by those who can do two things at one time. The emotional protests by victims do not always justify passing a new law. Rational, fair and quantified principles are at the very root of the American legislative process. Why do so many insist otherwise?

Frankly, I'm tired of fighting with emotional people who let the lack of facts get in the way of what they demand for the rest of us.

How about all those makeup artists, map readers, and cigarette lighters—especially the ones who discover the lit end has just dropped into their laps? Oh, and those burger eaters who eat and drink with both hands, therefore, steering the car with their elbow or knees. Ever see one of those? Why pick on cell phones?

Rest assured, sooner or later they'll have a law banning everything, because the stupid and very stupid among us cannot moderate their own behavior. As one friend of mine so wisely says, "ignorance can be fixed, but stupidity is forever." In order for the Nanny State to make it safer for us all, everyone else's liberties must be sacrificed until there are no more freedoms left to enjoy.

I used to believe that driving my car down the Interstate was one of the last, pure freedoms available to the average American citizen. However, since road rage, gas-guzzling SUV hatred, the ban on the dreaded cell phone, and all the other attentions paid to driving by the hand wringers and do-gooders, I've changed by mind.

All these driving related laws are nothing more than affirmative action for the stupid and slow thinking single-taskers who are jealous and intimidated by those of us who can chew gum and drive down the street at the same time.

Freedom on the road is becoming a distant memory.

There must be something left to do that's fun, where our Big Brother and Nanny government agencies are not listening and watching.

# PART II

# THE HARD-LEFT IN ACTION

# CHAPTER SIX—
# Go Ahead and Blame Clinton—I Do!

Is it true that national security professionals were blind-sided by the attacks on September 11, 2001? On the contrary, the attack on the World Trade Center towers and the Pentagon on September 11 was a continuation of an assault on the United States that began in 1993. Let's review the history.

## *WTC Attack #1*

In 1993, Osama bin Laden ordered the first attack on the World Trade Center with a truck bomb planted in the underground parking garage of one of the towers. The plan was for the powerful bomb to destroy the stability of one of the towers, causing it to topple into the other, thereby bringing both towers down.

The bomb was powerful, but few lives were lost, and at first examination most would have graded this terrorist attack as less than effective. After all, the terrorists wanted to inflict massive loss of life—that's how terrorists cause fear.

What was known, but not widely publicized, was that the truck also held a significant amount of poisonous gas which was supposed to have been drawn into the ventilating system of both buildings. If the blast had not extinguished the flame designed to generate the poisonous gas, many thousands would have died.

If the two towers had fallen that day in 1993, there probably would have been more deaths than on September 11, since people would not have had the time necessary to escape the buildings in the same way they did in 2001.

All this detail about the attack and what was supposed to happen was quickly made known to the Clinton administration. Early on, the investigation established a connection to Osama bin Laden. Yet Bill Clinton's decision to handle this horrific attack on our nation as an FBI investigation guaranteed that bin Laden would become more emboldened to engage in further terrorist activity.

## Somalia

Recall that U.S. troops were killed in Somalia when their Blackhawk helicopters were blasted from the sky by shoulder-launched surface-to-air missiles. Who supplied the arms and the training to Somalia's warlords? Osama bin Laden. Using the civil war in Somalia as a testing ground for his dream of engaging in war with the U.S., he proved to himself and his followers that he could wound us in significant ways.

Few knew of bin Laden's participation in Somalia and his contribution to the death and humiliation visited upon our military. But today, Osama bin Laden's henchmen brag and laugh that they shot down U.S. helicopters and then slit the throats of three U.S. servicemen before dragging them naked through the streets of Somalia.

And what did Clinton do about this? He bombed an aspirin factory and some sand dunes, which amounted to symbolic gesturing. Hardened terrorists were apparently not impressed with Clinton's popgun approach—they were only encouraged!

Back in the United States, all we knew was that a clueless Secretary of Defense, Les Aspin, turned down appeals from commanders on the scene to supply them with the proper equipment to undertake the mission ordered by the White House.

# Kibar Towers

After Somalia, there was one attack after another against U.S. interests and U.S. military, and yet Bill Clinton and his minions refused to connect the dots. Their response to each attack was to send in the FBI to conduct an investigation. The proper response would have been a military strike against Osama bin Laden.

Indeed, as I waited in the Green Room of the ABC studios in Washington in June of 1996 to be grilled by George Will, David Brinkley and Sam Donaldson about my new book—and to be accused of being a pathological liar by Clinton's flak, George Stephanopoulos—I watched as Secretary of Defense William Perry explained what the Clinton administration was going to do about the huge bomb which had just been exploded in Saudi Arabia. Kibar Towers, a housing unit filled with U.S. military personnel, had been destroyed and many were killed by the massive truck bomb.

And yet, Perry made no mention of the Clinton White House's strong suspicion that Osama bin Laden was behind the killing of so many American troops.

# The Attack on the U.S.S. Cole

When the U.S.S. Cole was bombed with the resulting death of many U.S. sailors, I wrote the following and received many notes from national security colleagues who told me that they were thinking the very same thing:

**White House Drops the Ball on U.S.S. Cole Warning**—October 25, 2000

"When it comes to the protection of national security, over and over again the Clinton/Gore White House drops the ball.

Many examples exist as ironclad proof of the incompetence of this Clinton/Gore administration in the area of national security that it seems useless to argue that this White House can, or ever will, get anything right.

Of course, there are those who are still hoping to this day that they will grow into the job. But, security professionals do not live on hope, or guess, or gamble with the lives of others.

I don't think the Clinton/Gore bunch will ever get it when it comes to the seriousness of the threats against this nation—they only have about 90 days left to get up to speed.

Meanwhile, millions of our brave young service men and women are in harm's way, at the mercy of those who are too often short on good decisions, and shorter still on high performance.

I know good journalism requires examples of what I'm claiming, but frankly I'm so sick and tired of those blockheads in the White House that I can't bear to list their many serious screw-ups again. Besides, if concerned citizens don't know about the Clinton White House by now—if they haven't reached a conclusion by now—what could I or anyone else write to help them make up their minds?

In the *Washington Times* we learned that there were serious warnings given by the NSA about a terrorist attack soon to be launched against our citizens in a specific part of the world—that part of the world where the U.S.S. Cole was to be refueled. But the warnings were not passed on to the Navy in a timely manner. By the time the warnings made their way to the proper parties, many had already met a horrible, tragic fate.

I know from my time in the FBI that "hot" information of this kind, bearing on a terrorist act about to be perpetrated, would have been immediately sent to the White House so that officials within the National Security Council and the President's inner circle could immediately deal with whatever threat was raised.

True security pros would have understood the need for immediate and decisive action—to pass on this serious warning to the U.S. Navy ships in the area. We have taken an absence from excellence for so long that it's difficult to remember a time when things actually did work swiftly and smoothly.

When did we agree as a country that third-rate performance was good enough?

We'll now wait for the predictable congressional inquiry, but I'll wager that Sandy Burger and his top-level NSC staffers were absent from the premises when the warnings came in—probably off to some Gore Campaign fund-raiser, or perhaps hobnobbing with some Chinese generals at a hot Washington night spot.

When I worked there I had a hard time finding any serious people in the Clinton/Gore White House. Sex, drugs and Rock and Roll has a way of distracting folks from serious business, I guess.

I know that sounds so cynical, but is there a single person left in this country that does not have an absolute right to their cynicism about this seriously flawed group of La La Land people from the incomprehensible, dysfunctional Sixties?

The FBI sent 100 special agents to the other side of the globe to investigate crimes related to the attack on the U.S.S. Cole. How about sending about 50 FBI special agents down to the Clinton White House where some of the biggest crimes of our time have been committed?"

At the time I wrote that essay, there were many who would have labeled me as too extreme, I suppose. I wonder what they would say today.

## *Waiting for the next "Pearl Harbor"?*

Bill Clinton has been overheard whining that he won't enjoy the legacy of a wartime president as George W. Bush will. With all that has happened and all that we now know, doesn't it make you wonder whether Bill Clinton was waiting for bin Laden to commit a massive terror attack in this country, so that he, Bill Clinton, could then emerge as the hero of the moment?

Clinton had plenty of warning about what was coming. Bin Laden had already ordered one attack on the World Trade Center. Bill Clinton had all the intelligence resources of the CIA and FBI, as well as the NSA and foreign intelligence services. As time goes by, we learn that Bill Clinton knew a lot about bin Laden and what he was planning to do to us, but he did little to stop him.

Under a previous Democratic president, our nation didn't get engaged in an obviously worthwhile war to contain similar terrorists who were threatening the world. It took an attack on Pearl Harbor to force us to become engaged.

Then, we were shocked and outraged by the Japanese attack, and the population moved swiftly to support their president and strong U.S. military action.

Many suspect Roosevelt knew the Japanese were going to attack us, but waited so he would not have to convince U.S. citizens that we should commit U.S. forces to World War II. He never confessed that this was his intent, so we will never know.

Was Clinton waiting for what appears to be the inevitable "second Pearl Harbor" attack on our country by bin Laden? Could this attack have been prevented by swift and massive military action ordered by Bill Clinton after the attack on the U.S.S. Cole?

We'll probably never know what hides in the deep recesses of this black-hearted, Hard-Left sociopath, but less complex Machiavellian plots have been hatched by simpler men, and these plots have been just as deadly. Was Clinton Machiavellian in his approach to most every issue facing him as our commander in chief? I believe the answer is an obvious, "Yes!"

One thing seems clear: Bill Clinton never lifted a finger to help anyone or do anything that was not in his own best interest.

In fact, Bill Clinton is the most selfish man I have ever investigated—and in my mind, that makes him a suspect of having knowledge of the coming deadly attack.

## Down Clinton's Rabbit Hole

For those people who like more detail, let's examine Clinton's political wanderings on terrorism a little more closely. (Maybe he should have stopped and asked for directions!)

Marketing gurus and psychologists understand that harmless radicals can be made to appear dangerous in the eyes of the general population if a PR campaign is clever enough. I submit that a storm of news articles, complemented by a choir of willing TV pundits expressing alarm and outrage, can demonize any group—regardless of their true potential to harm others or negatively impact national security.

And who holds great sway in determining the media's focus on alleged radicals from the opposite party's fringe, whether they choose to exercise this power or not? I believe a case can be made that this power falls, in large part, into the hands of whatever political party occupies the Oval Office.

After the demonization process is complete, the full forces of the federal law enforcement community—armed with new powers and fat budgets from a compliant Congress as a knee-jerk reaction—can then move forward to eliminate the threat. The party in power can launch a political jihad to wound the opposition party if the allegations are broad enough and repeated often enough. Even though a fringe radical group has nothing at all to do with a legitimate, mainstream political agenda, their over-the-top statements and actions can be made to look like party ideology.

An honest political party in power would never stoop to such dangerous and underhanded tactics, unless that party had nothing left of value to offer the voters. Why would such tactics be dangerous? Because, while the media and the nation are absorbed with the phony threat being hyped by the administration in power, real threats will be ignored.

In the meantime, the real terrorists can grow in strength and numbers.

## *Case in Point #1: Waco, Texas*

After taking office in 1993, Bill Clinton's Department of Justice, led by Janet Reno, convinced the nation that a rag-tag group of religious fanatics in Texas, cobbled together by a man exhibiting behavior not seen since the Jonestown massacre, were in a position to break out and threaten vast numbers of innocent citizens.

We were never told exactly how these fanatics would do this, and close examination has proven the absurdity of the claims, as this group was nothing more than a small band of deranged, confused citizens. In fact, a case can be made that many of these so-called members were held against their will by plain old-fashioned brainwashing, including verbal and physical abuse.

The Branch Davidians, living far away from any neighbors on a compound near Waco, Texas, had accumulated a stockpile of arms, some illegal. The ATF had obtained search warrants and were attempting to serve those warrants on the compound when a gunfight broke out. We have since learned that the ATF could have served the warrants in a safe, peaceful manner since David Koresh, the leader of this sect, often went to the nearby town alone. Both sides claim the other side fired the first shots. The nation cringed as four federal officers were slain by Davidian gunfire. The raid was broadcast on TV because the ATF had wanted to achieve a public relations coup, but their incompetence caused a chain of events that led to a massive loss of life.

The Clinton White House, suffering criticism from the botched and deadly raid, dumped the case on the FBI, who then sent in their Hostage Rescue Team (HRT) for the purpose of arresting the murderers of the ATF agents. Led by George Stephanopoulos, the Clinton White House went into full spin-mode to justify the killings. In order to do this, they had to paint the Branch Davidians as dangerous terrorists.

In fact, this group consisted of perhaps a dozen men, heavily armed, effectively isolated far from the nearest town, totally surrounded by hundreds of highly trained, well equipped federal, state and local law enforcement officials. In other words, they posed no threat, except to themselves and the law enforcement officers who held them in virtual captivity. There was no reason to storm the compound, unless it was to rescue hostages. If that was the goal, the FBI sure had a deadly way of going about it.

There is no doubt that there were dangerous men inside that compound, but the majority were women and children. Regardless of the obvious innocence of most of the complex's occupants, the Clinton White House worked in concert with a willing media to demonize all who were unfortunate enough to fall under the spell of Koresh—a modern-day Jim Jones.

Instead of treating the women and children as innocent captives, at risk from a forced group-suicide, the Clinton Justice Department pushed for an early end to the standoff through the use of military-like violence, led by a former tank commander who was heading up the FBI's HRT. The extensive dangers of the raid were carefully explained to Janet Reno and relayed to the Clinton White House, but a green light was given anyway.

In order to justify this extraordinary level of violence by federal authorities on U.S. soil, it was necessary to dehumanize all who were behind those flimsy walls—not a difficult task. All the occupants were religious fanatics and most were white. They were "loony Christians" led by an "angry white man" whose top lieutenants were also angry white men. And, they had exercised their Second Amendment rights—they were armed.

In other words, they were part of the Vast Right Wing. According to the Clinton White House and Janet Reno's Justice Department, this was reason enough to allow a tank attack, crashing through walls and spraying large doses of toxic tear gas at children.

When the FBI finally brought an end to the standoff in Waco, more than 20 children had died in a flaming murder-suicidal tragedy. But the Branch Davidians had been demonized so effectively by the White House and the media that many Americans seemed confused and didn't know whether to cheer or cry about the loss of innocent life. The stand-off was over; the immediate threat was removed, but a new, so-called major threat to our nation had been revealed:

The new threat was "angry white men," who were part of a Vast Right Wing Conspiracy.

## Case in Point #2: Oklahoma City, Oklahoma

Two years after Waco, two young men, apparently seriously demented but not aligned with any known political party anyone knows of, blew up a federal office building in Oklahoma City.

Although there are a growing number of individuals who claim that Timothy McVeigh and Terry Nichols acted in concert with individuals described as Middle Easterners, we were told that the bombing was, once again, all about angry white men aligned with others in this country loosely known as the Militia.

What we know now is that the federal government knew that a few individuals were planning to blow up the federal building—not because they were angry white males, but because one of their associates was about to be put to the needle on death row!

Sadly, the Clinton's Department of Justice knew of the plan, but failed to alert the proper authorities. Anyway, it was politically better to blame the Vast Right Wing.

FBI agents fanned out to discover new pockets of religious fanatics, abortion clinic protesters and old men wearing flannel shirts with red suspenders who were oddly intent on protecting the Constitution and the Bill of Rights.

Meanwhile, a terrorist attack of a real kind was underway, designed to take down the Twin Towers of New York's World Trade Center. Osama bin Laden, a real terrorist, moved his pawns into place, ready to inflict catastrophic damage while Janet Reno opened sweeping investigations designed to identify and arrest a vast network of Christians engaged in a conspiracy to commit violent acts at abortion clinics—a network that never existed.

Years later, what does the U.S. government have to show for the tremendous investment of resources used to identify, catalogue and maintain FBI files on thousands of law-abiding, decent Americans who simply loved their Constitution and Bill of Rights? Exactly nothing! Clinton perceived a Right Wing threat for exactly what it was—a true national movement to oust a disgusting, failed and reckless leader from national office.

The Right was a political threat of the highest order, and Bill Clinton understood the gravity of that threat.

An incompetent and dishonest Clinton, distracted by young interns, a wrathful wife and determined political opponents, either failed to recognize the scope of danger bin Laden posed to our national security, or chose for his own Machiavellian reasons to ignore it, leaving us vulnerable to even more devastating attacks.

Clinton remained distracted, mired in his own muck, as Saddam Hussein chased our inspectors out of Iraq. Now we'll pick up Clinton's Iraq "tab" as well, and it will be paid for with more American blood.

Some say the Clintons were so smart, but decent, smart people don't demonize others as terrorists simply because they want to maintain power and privilege. They don't want it, or need it, that badly. Only dishonest and dull-witted political hacks fear the loyal opposition.

Behold the Clinton legacy—it is truly terrible.


# *Is "PC" Dead?*

Because our own government would not tell us the entire truth about Osama bin Laden and his plans for our destruction, we were caught completely off guard on September 11, 2001.

Because Bill Clinton and his Hard-Left pacifist friends were loath to send in the military and instead chose to use an ineffective squad of FBI agents, this country was lulled into thinking that the threat facing us was much less than it really was.

Citizens of this great land would have supported military action against bin Laden, but first they would have needed to be educated about the high level of threat. This is one of the biggest failings of Bill Clinton and his administration: to properly educate the American people about the nature of the threat Osama bin Laden represented to this country.

These were murderous, crazed lunatics, but somebody in the Clinton administration apparently saw terrorists in a different light. After all, didn't they pardon Puerto Rican terrorists? Murder, bombing, and torture isn't so bad, I guess, when the terrorists are promoting a movement seen in harmony with your own political beliefs. After all, isn't everything—including terrorists—relative?

What is it about a religion that prescribes mutilation of a woman's genitals and the stoning of a woman suspected of adultery that bothers squeamish people like me? The fact that women are literally treated like cattle and can be beaten in public and killed in private is unacceptable. This cannot be passed off as simply a cultural or religious difference.

Why didn't we—why didn't Bill Clinton—conclude that angry, hostile, irrational, violent behavior could someday be turned upon us?

We did not need a president to "feel our pain" or hold our hand; we needed a president to move our hand—to move many of our powerful hands to strike Osama bin Laden.

For that reason, our new president, George W. Bush, got stuck with the job of educating the public, and what a great job he's doing!

President Bush has set the nation on a course starkly different from the Clinton administration's approach of investigating and indicting terrorist perpetrators. Most agree today that Clinton's response was a deadly failure, but many involved in the protection of national security knew it was a disastrous course before it became U.S. policy. Those who objected to the Clintonista's new world order tactics were immediately scorned.

These terrorists said they would attack us, they did attack us, and we had no protections in place to stop them. Two decades of law enforcement taught me that criminal violence has no logic. Terrorism is political-criminal violence, a brutal attempt to seize power when verbal persuasion is not working.

In other words, when lies are not enough, you blow up people.

While Bill Clinton and his crowd expended enormous energy demonizing law abiding U.S. citizens for wanting to own guns—a guaranteed right in the U.S. Constitution—religious extremists were arming themselves with the latest military armaments and technology. While Bill Clinton wagged a finger at us for our anger at his frivolity in the Oval Office, terrorists were plotting, bombing and killing our citizens and striking our military installations and equipment.

The politically correct vision of "the man from Hope" (a man who actually loathed the military) was to turn bombers into butterflies. Many of the Cold-Warriors that didn't buy into his hookah pipe dream were harassed into early retirement.

However, there were plenty of people who were in perfect lockstep with Clinton. Some of these same people appear on TV today and tell us what we should do next. If they had a clue about what to do, why didn't they do it when they had the chance and the power?

When Bill Clinton assumed command, his first concern was making the U.S. military safe—for gays and lesbians, that is.

Republicans in the White House may be bad for welfare programs, but nobody—I repeat: nobody—can ever make the case that a Republican president has ever been soft on national defense. The Hard-Left is infamous for the creation of crises and false choices. They have led us to believe that if you have a strong military and maintain a strong intelligence capability, somehow you cannot inoculate children or rid neighborhoods of toxic waste.

Now we face real biological terror, and you can't get much more toxic than the site which used to be the World Trade Center.

Did political correctness die along with our collective naiveté on September 11? Try speaking these words:

"Tighten up the U.S. borders! Arrest or detain any illegal immigrants who may have had a part in, or knowledge about, the terrible event on September 11. Bomb any country that encourages attacks against the U.S., and kill their leaders. Rebuild the U.S. military. Report suspicious activity. Take a careful look at those who are joining you on your next airplane ride, then go ahead and plan violent acts against any who attempt to take over the flight.

And carry your wonderful cell phone at all times—even in your SUV—dial 911 when you see something that alarms you. Pay attention to what's really important—alertness may save your life or the life of your neighbor."

Are you at odds with anything you just read aloud? Maybe PC is dead! After thirty long years of wandering in a hazy Woodstock Wilderness, it's possible that we've become a nation managed by adults. The Hard-Left PC crowd has suddenly lost all credibility.

Good riddance to the Hard Left, flower power, and all the other nonsense that have now made America a dangerous place to live.

But of course, they aren't gone—they've just gone underground or have taken new jobs to rebuild their tattered credibility.

# *Mainstream Media Covers for Clinton and Friends*

I was not surprised to see the *Washington Post* defending the hapless Clinton administration. But what was especially galling was the label the *Post* chose to describe eight years of misuse of resources masquerading as real responses to actual terrorist threats against our nation.

The *Post* actually had the nerve to call Clinton's fiddling, "Clinton's War on Terrorism."

When I first read the headline containing this outrage, I laughed, but then I got angry. There was no "Clinton War on Terrorism"! But, there were many wars waged by our former commander in chief. There was the war on decency. There was the war on our military, when Clinton and his cronies and croni-ettes attempted to feminize our armed forces, and coerce our warriors into accepting both women and men with conflicting gender preferences.

Then, there were the wars on drug companies, and doctors, and Big Tobacco and Microsoft. And, who will ever forget the enormous resources brought to bear against the Radical Right, in the wake of the Republican take-over of Congress in 1994?

The Vast Right Wing, touted as a danger to national security, provided yet another war for the Democratic Party.

Meanwhile, Clinton banished the CIA director from the White House, and made it clear he had no real interest in foreign affairs. The joke going around the White House at the time when a nut crashed a plane onto the South Lawn, was that the pilot was CIA Director Woolsey, trying to get an appointment with the president.

Informed citizens know all of this, and more, and will not be fooled by the attempts made by the *Washington Post* or any other of Clinton's liberal media friends to airbrush history.

Richard Cohen, a particularly obnoxious Hard-Lefty who writes for the *Post,* recently claimed the reason Clinton could not wage an effective war against Osama bin Laden was because he was too busy waging war with his wife, with Kenneth Starr, Bob Barr, Paula Jones, Linda Tripp, Monica Lewinsky, Kathleen Willey, the Vast Right Wing Conspiracy, and...yours truly.

According to Cohen, we were attacked on September 11 because decent Americans complained loudly about Bill Clinton's disgusting conduct performed on our White House Oval Office rug with a young woman—a government employee. He was involved in activities most Americans would find shameful and beneath contempt. Clinton's attempts to hide this conduct caused one of the most damaging insults to the minds of our nation's youth as they were forced to watch and listen to a president attempt to explain what sex isn't and what it is.

Our nation was also humiliated to learn that a president would lie under oath to save his own political skin. Even the hated Nixon never did that.

And the *Post* and Cohen contend that all of this is our fault, not Clinton's.

## *Where are Freeh and the Others in All This?*

While I hold Clinton mainly responsible for the catastrophic damage to our country on September 11, 2001, he did not work alone. Where's Louis Freeh? Most of the planning by Osama bin Laden for

September 11 happened on Freeh's watch. Why isn't former FBI Director Louis Freeh being called to explain the sorry condition of the FBI, the agency that Robert Mueller inherited just two weeks before our nation was so savagely attacked?

And, where's former FBI Director William Sessions? President Bill Clinton fired Judge Sessions in 1993, and when he was asked by journalist Christopher Ruddy of NewsMax.com why he was fired, Judge Sessions replied that it was because he objected to Clinton's politicizing of the FBI.

Could Judge Sessions tell us anything about FBI prohibitions against racial profiling?

Come to think of it, where's Janet Reno in the current lineup? Didn't she run the Justice Department for eight years while the FBI atrophied and the INS and other agencies under her jurisdiction got out of control? Perhaps she could drive her little red truck up here from Florida and lend some help in finding out why this terror has happened to us.

U.S. senators called George Tenet to the stand numerous times to explain serious shortcomings at the CIA. But, where's James Woolsey, the former CIA director who has made no secret of his disgust for the Clinton administration? Wasn't it Woolsey who could not *buy* a meeting with President Clinton? (Funny, isn't it? Monica Lewinsky could get appointments, but the CIA director could not. What did Monica have that CIA Director Woolsey did not have? A beret?)

And where's former CIA Director John M. Deutch, the one who Clinton had to pardon because he was accused of mishandling secrets on his CIA laptop, which he left unsecured at home while the maids dusted his furniture.

By any chance, did the maid wear a head scarf?

Under the leadership—if you can call it that—of Transportation Secretary Norman Y. Mineta, the FAA, a dysfunctional joke, was so far-gone that whistleblowers who recognized the dangerous practices of the agency stood in line to reveal what they knew. Is Mineta going to be publicly questioned, or would the U.S. Senate consider that racial profiling?

Where are the U.S. senators on the witness list for post September 11 congressional hearings? How many senators were warned by career professionals who became whistleblowers that national security was in a state of disaster—including the White House, where dysfunction really counts?

The FBI and CIA told Clinton's National Security Counsel all about the coming storm. What were *they* doing about it? Perhaps they were too busy feting Irish terrorist Gerry Adams in the White House, or planning photo ops for Hillary in New York with Mrs. Arafat, or advising President Clinton on the pluses and minuses of pardoning Puerto Rican terrorists—those who killed some of New York's finest—our beloved First Responders.

I am amazed at how Louis Freeh and Janet Reno have been able to escape answering for their remarkable misuse of Department of Justice and FBI resources to chase the wrong suspects. How is it that they deserve such immunity?

Long before the national argument concerning who knew what about Osama bin Laden and when they knew it, I wrote the following report. This may serve to convince some skeptics that there are many of us in the business of protecting national security who saw right through Bill and Hillary Clinton. But, why are so many so gullible? Here's the report.

## *Death by the Hard-Left*

"Several days have passed since the most outrageous act of terrorism in the history of the world occurred. The clearance of the wreckage has just begun. Meanwhile, thousands of innocent victims lie beneath smoldering rubble. It will take weeks until the last girders are lifted from the sub-basements of the World Trade Center buildings in New York City. We weep for the victims and pray that more of them will be found alive.

But there will be no peace; and there will be no rest. Rescue workers toil to bring to us what they can, but most victims were reduced to ash or destroyed beyond recognition by the compressions, the explosions and the inferno that followed.

Fall rains will wash American blood and ashes down into the storm drains of New York City, and the essence of American lives lost will move down the Hudson River to the Atlantic Ocean and be sent by the ocean currents around the globe. Their innocent blood will someday reach the shores of nations who nurture and harbor terrorists, to join the bombs that we'll soon send there to extract our retribution.

We now learn that these animals were trained on our soil. They attended flight training schools in our country; they lived among us as our neighbors. Their children attended schools with our children.

They came across U.S. borders with papers that allowed easy entry and exit. There are hundreds—perhaps thousands—of these terrorists here today. About 50 of them have surfaced to carry out these evils acts. The rest await orders from abroad.

I submit that these terrorists enjoyed more freedom and liberty than we did. After all, while we were being questioned about our baggage, x-rayed and searched, real criminals came and went as they pleased. And then, these murderers boarded jetliners with their knives, phony bombs and threats. Grandmothers and teenagers presented photo IDs and put their keys and change in a dish, while extremely dangerous men carried on long-distance conversations about jet fuel and potential body counts.

I hope now we will realize that combating terrorism with feel-good, symbolic gestures won't work. Perhaps a significant number of our citizens are fooled, but the terrorists are smart. They laugh at our feeble attempts to create the illusion of safety.

They drive effortlessly through our cities and towns and eat our cheeseburgers, while we dodge concrete barriers and walk around black, metal pylons. We must go miles out of our way so that we can get from one end of the District of Columbia to the other because Bill Clinton closed Pennsylvania Avenue to achieve a symbolic security everyone knew was as flimsy as an eggshell.

We, as a nation, were led to believe that the Hard-Left Liberals' way of dealing with terrorism was preferable to the Conservatives' gut feelings. My friends know that the only effective way to deal with an obvious threat like the one we're facing is to squash these bugs like a farmer would apply his boot to a scorpion—and for the same reasons: if you don't kill the damn thing, sooner or later, you or one of your loved ones will be stung.

We were even given a new set of enemies to consider. Call it a distraction, but we were told that the real threat was not from some Islamic fundamentalists who vowed to commit terrorist acts to bring us to our knees. No, Bill Clinton and Janet Reno and their friends on Capitol Hill and in the media spoke as one voice about the home-grown threat posed by church-going Americans, protesting partial-birth abortion.

And then they demonized well-organized militia groups who complained loudly about Clinton's liberal agenda. They were considered suspicious because they expressed absolute disgust for our commander in chief, while noticing Clinton's ignorance of the constitutional protections guaranteed to us all.

These same bearded, flannel-shirted suspicious characters are now running the backhoes and girder cutters in New York City, working around the clock until they drop from exhaustion, attempting to do what real Americans have always done.

Meanwhile, the girly-men Liberals and their strident molls scratch their heads and wonder how and why September 11, 2001, happened. After all, weren't they nice to these terrorists? Didn't they display the correct amount of tolerance for another peoples' religious beliefs?

Didn't Hillary Clinton actually embrace and kiss Arafat's wife?

Yes, she did—and this is the thanks she gets! Why, Hillary even helped release Puerto Rican terrorist bombers in a symbolic display of healing and forgiveness! Talk about being blind sided after you've gone out of your way to be nice!

Hard-Left Liberals were not the only ones blind sided. Apparently the FBI and CIA were absolutely clueless that the terrorists were here and had a well-organized, well-funded plan to commit the worst act of terrorism in our nation's history.

Is it possible that the FBI was too busy keeping an eye on so-called domestic terrorism to notice? Could it be that the CIA was unable to penetrate this awful plan because a former Clinton appointee, who happened to be the CIA director, decided that CIA agents could no longer recruit spies who were suspected of illegal activity?

We are a country confused about who our enemies are, and what we are to do about them. Until now, we have not been able to distinguish a real threat from a paper tiger.

Even though our embassies have been bombed, our Navy attacked, and our allies terrorized by the same religious fanatics, we have been unable to come to a solution. That is, until now. Now we get it. Now we see what's real versus what's concocted for political gain.

Now we will do the real work—the work of men: protecting our citizens against all threats, foreign and domestic.

For eight long years the Hard-Left Liberals partied—and they have run up an enormous tab. Thousands of American lives have been cashiered for the Hard-Left's asinine, childish ideas about national security. The warnings about their Age of Aquarius approach to the protection of our lives were being sounded as early as 1993. Clinton's participation in the unraveling of our nation's security was well known by the summer of 1996.

Still, so many of our citizens preferred to believe Bill Clinton.

There were so many terrorist events along the way, some of them terrible to behold, but nothing was as horrible as September 11. Nevertheless, many Americans had already died at the hands of Islamic fanatics residing on foreign shores, coming and going from the U.S. whenever they pleased, photo IDs in hand.

The Hard-Left Liberals' solution was always to make nice with terrorists while whittling away at our liberties and freedoms with symbolic rent-a-cop checkpoints, laughable metal detectors and meaningless photo ID checks.

Thank God, adults have returned to our White House. Now, if only they can find a way to keep the Hard-Left Liberals at bay while a man's work finally gets done. Too late for the victims in New York, Virginia and Pennsylvania, I'm sorry to say.

Excuse me if I absent myself from the national political group-hug that's currently underway. I believe the Hard-Left Liberals are largely responsible for much of what happened September 11, and may God forgive them. (But I won't.)

My job and the job of all Conservatives now is to keep the Hard-Left out of power as long as humanly possible. Our country is not safe when the Hard-Left is in power.

How much more evidence do we need?"

That's what I believed just days after September 11, 2001, and all that I've learned since then has done nothing but strengthen my beliefs.

Americans should use common sense and go ahead and blame Bill Clinton and his Hard-Left comrades. It feels good; it feels right, and it's the right thing to do.

# CHAPTER SEVEN—
# How to Fix the Once Mighty FBI

## *Politics and the FBI is Nothing New*

The secret to fixing what's wrong with the FBI can be summed up in one word: Politics! Politics, that is political correctness, has altered the management and general population of the FBI so that now it's nearly impossible to discipline special agents.

Discipline is at the heart of running any effective and efficient organization.

Politics also controls what the FBI investigates. Agents are told how to spend their time by management, who in turn are told by their director how to spend agents' time. The FBI Director is told by the U.S. Department of Justice what crimes or terrorist organizations should be addressed. In turn, the Attorney General is told by the White House what's to be emphasized, and what should be de-emphasized.

And, although there are several oversight committees on Capitol Hill that are supposed to make sure the FBI resources are used wisely, it's a fact that representatives and senators are guilty of using the FBI to investigate pet violations, such as environmental issues, or social issues like deadbeat dads, a favorite whipping-boy for feminists.

The FBI's troubles did not begin with the Clinton administration, and certainly didn't end when Clinton and Gore left office. But, eight years of Clinton/Gore/Reno mismanagement and misuse of FBI resources left the agency in tatters. No new president, no matter how well briefed on the FBI's ills could ever undo eight years worth of damage in one, two, or even three years.

Ironically, it may be the FBI failures surfaced after the horrible attacks on our country on September 11, 2001, that will ultimately save the once vaunted agency. The Bush family has been steadfast fans of the FBI—I know this from personal conversations I've had with people close to both presidents. Although some like me were convinced the bureau had serious problems, the Bush family was not so convinced.

But September 11 brought every agency's flaws to the surface, and the FBI was perhaps spot-lighted more than some. In my way, I attempted to surface FBI shortcomings in a very public way with a *Wall Street Journal* editorial in the summer of 1996. Here is the op-ed I wrote in its entirety.

# *The Character Issue and the FBI*

Bob Dole and Jack Kemp won loud applause from the mainstream media for refusing to make President Clinton's character an issue in recent debates. I believe the media are wrong. Character does matter—profoundly. The consequences of its absence in the current administration can be seen in the politicization of the FBI, an agency I am proud to have served.

When I was writing my book, *Unlimited Access: An FBI Agent Inside the Clinton White House*, my working title was *Character Matters*. I was frightened by a pattern of ignoring long-established procedures that ensured the good character of those who have access to the White House. I believed—and still believe—that the White House's laxity is a threat to national security. It's also a threat to the honesty of America's political debate. How can President Clinton's claim that "I hate drugs" be allowed to pass when his administration has routinely granted White House passes to employees with a recent history of drug use?

The mainstream media chose to ignore the serious issues raised in my book. Journalists have treated the book as if it had been thoroughly discredited—"packed with gossipy, unverified tidbits," one *Washington Post* news story said. In fact, my book was more thoroughly sourced than the *Post*'s Watergate coverage, much of which was based on a key source who remains unidentified 23 years later.

Before I landed what used to be an honorable and enjoyable assignment for a senior FBI agent—serving at the White House—I was assigned complex criminal investigations in major cities throughout America. I testified in numerous trials and before countless grand juries, and presented the facts I had gathered and documented to more than 100 Assistant U.S. Attorneys. Not once in 20 years was I ever criticized for the way in which I gathered evidence. Instead, I was consistently awarded for it. The national media have completely disregarded this long record of service; neither the *New York Times* nor the *Washington Post* has even bothered to review my book.

Outside of the major media, however, someone must believe. My book has been on the bestseller lists of the *New York Times, The Washington Post* and elsewhere for the past three months. My publisher says 410,000 copies are now in print. Having been blacklisted by the networks and major print media, we went straight to the grass roots via radio talk shows. Hundreds of producers and hosts called to seek my interview. I was amazed to learn from the hosts and callers just how informed the American people were about the antics of the Clinton administration. There are even "I believe Gary Aldrich" buttons which are given away faster than they can be made.

I was there. I saw and heard the things I wrote about it. What I saw in the Clinton White House scared me, and I had been an FBI agent for 26 years. I believed in my sources then, and I still do today. Much of the information in my book—information that is being confirmed almost weekly now, even by the national press—is from White House sources who must remain anonymous for fear of losing their jobs. But I had worked with them for years, and they had been accurate before. They were trusted people, credible enough to use in any search warrant; they told me about serious and serial scandals at the Clinton White House.

In seeking to dismiss the bulk of this testimony, my critics have seized on one incident, the claim that Mr. Clinton has eluded his Secret Service detail to sneak out of the White House at night. To my everlasting regret, one of my sources for part of this story was a journalist with a competing book; I may never be able to prove that the president went to the Marriott Hotel those nights. But I double sourced the story of the backseat-blanket-limo rides; it was observed by a White House employee. I was satisfied that the president went somewhere without his Secret Service agents, and the national security implications of that worried me a lot.

In hindsight, perhaps I should have anticipated the attacks about sources, but it would have been hard to anticipate the orchestrated campaign described by Fred Barnes in *The Weekly Standard.* He reported that the White House had been pressuring news organizations to keep me off the air. According to Mr. Barnes, White House Press Secretary Michael McCurry threatened to punish ABC, for example, by canceling the president's planned interview with Barbara Walters if the network went ahead with plans to interview me on *This Week with David Brinkley.* In the end, I was allowed to appear on the program, but I was subjected to a barrage of hostile questions based on a critique of my book that George Stephanopoulos and two other White House aides had provided before the show. After *Brinkley,* Mr. Stephanopoulos reportedly boasted of my book: "We killed it." Sure enough, I was shut out of the mainstream media: NBC and CNN both canceled plans to interview me.

It turned out that the White House had a long time to prepare for its assault on *Unlimited Access,* for it had improperly received a copy of the manuscript from the FBI. When current or retired FBI agents write books they are required to submit them, prior to publication, to the bureau for review. The FBI is supposed to make sure that the author is not revealing any material that is private, classified or dangerous to national security.

But when I sent my manuscript to the FBI, the bureau's chief counsel, Howard Shapiro, forwarded it straight to the White House. Mr. Shapiro then attacked me directly, ultimately recommending that the Justice Department begin proceedings to withhold royalties from the sale of my book.

When I submitted the manuscript to the FBI for review, I expected to see agents from headquarters at my door to interview me about the mismanagement within the bureau that I had witnessed. But I was never contacted. Instead of attempting to find out whether the FBI was in the dumpster due to the corruption of this White House, Mr. Shapiro acted to protect Bill and Hillary Clinton, even at the expense of dedicated career agents' reputations. Along with his response to my book, Mr. Shapiro has questioned the integrity of my former partner, Dennis Sculembrine, after Mr. Sculembrine reported that former White House Counsel Bernard Nussbaum said Mrs. Clinton had wanted Craig Livingstone as her security chief.

Mr. Shapiro's conduct raises serious questions about the politicization of the FBI. What separates the U.S. from most other countries is a system of law enforcement that is as immune from partisan political pressures as is humanly possible. Of course, even in America there is an inexorable pull toward the politicization of law enforcement.

Before Mr. Shapiro arrived, the FBI counsel had always been an FBI agent/attorney who had worked his way up through the ranks. Attorney General Janet Reno heralded Mr. Shapiro's arrival as "wonderful," suggesting that getting FBI mentality out of the front office of the FBI was a good thing. The fact is that Mr. Shapiro represents a trend toward the politicization of a law enforcement agency that, for the sake of our democracy, desperately needs to keep its head above the political water. The FBI must regain its reputation as well as its sense of internal pride. A good place to begin would be to fire Mr. Shapiro and insist on replacing him with an agent/attorney who places the best interests of the bureau above narrow political concerns.

After all, it is the mission, always the mission, which keeps an agent on the straight and narrow—that, and the Constitution and a very thick FBI manual. If the mission is to keep company with the high and mighty over at the White House, the two missions must, and always will, conflict—all the more so when the president doesn't feel accountable for his character and that of his administration.

## Political Courage: The PC We Should Support

It's difficult to make a case that the FBI has not been politicized. But the degree of impact that politics has in the day of an average FBI special agent depends a lot on political courage.

Minneapolis Special Agent Coleen Rowley raised the issue of political correctness in her now famous memo to the FBI director when she suggested that the reason a warrant was not issued to search the computer hard drive of Moussaoui was because FBI Headquarters managers were worried about "racial profiling." In the crafting and distribution of her memo, Special Agent Rowley found the courage to say what a lot of others were already thinking.

Many were impressed with agent Rowley's courage. In fact, *Time Magazine* editors were so impressed they selected her as one of three whistleblowers worthy of gracing their cover, as "Women of the year." I've spent a little personal time with agent Rowley and her husband—and found them to be both genuine and courageous. They express Traditional American Values which must make feminists quite nervous.

How is it that Rowley became an FBI agent without adopting Hard-Left ideology? The fact is, most of the female agents in the FBI today are hard-core Conservative—somehow they don't need the National Organization for Women to succeed.

We haven't heard from the FBI managers who stand accused of serious inaction by Rowley, but did she make a valid claim? Has political correctness (PC) gripped the FBI so that it constrains the normal law enforcement functions that might otherwise keep us safer?

I would contend that PC hampers the FBI no more or less than it hampers the average PTA president or minister or priest. In fact, if we look around and listen, we would have to conclude that many of us have become PC to one degree or another, and those who have refused to cave in to this dysfunctional group think mentality seem odd to us—curiously out of step.

The fact is, we have been scolded so much by the PC Police that we have nearly lost our precious rights of free speech. Think of all the things you are no longer "allowed" to say; the list is long. Think of all the immoral, immodest, crude conduct you are no longer "allowed" to object to out of fear that you may offend somebody. Today it seems that just about anything goes, as long as it's not illegal—and the Hard-Left is working on *that, too!*

Some would contend that the Hard-Left, finding itself unable to force changes through the courts, has turned to the media to get their wacky agenda forced through. In a recent morning newspaper, for ex-ample, a loony college professor contended that a monkey is as smart as his four-year old child, and, therefore, the monkey should enjoy the same civil rights as his child. The question is, how smart is the newspaper editor who thought this news was news?

Nevertheless, today's laughable news item has a good chance of becoming tomorrow's PC rule against making fun of animal behavior or repeating monkey jokes. That's because when we consider how all the other agenda items managed to become cemented into our cultural rule book, we may also remember that we dismissed previous silly notions and stood silent as the Hard-Left marched the agenda forward, right into the PC handbook. Nobody can claim innocence in this regard—unless they have the intellect of a monkey.

So, if we don't stand up to PC, how are FBI managers and line agents supposed to fend it off? They're only acting the way they think we want them to act.

Another example of PC becoming deadly hits closer to home. It's about screening airline passengers for signs of terrorist activity. The ACLU has filed a lawsuit against several major airline carriers because in the days immediately following the deadly September 11, 2001, at-tack against our country, four Middle Eastern young men were escorted off of scheduled airline flights because the other passengers refused to fly with them. All that the passengers wanted was the security of knowing that these young men were not part of another attack.

The ACLU objected to this, claiming that no matter what, there could not be racial profiling! We might conclude that no one in the ACLU's leadership lost relatives in the World Trade Towers, or in the Pentagon bombing, or on the hijacked flights, or else we'd have to con-clude they are simply crazy!

Nevertheless, the ACLU pressed forward with their lawsuit be-cause four young men were inconvenienced for a few hours and had their feelings hurt.

Is it any wonder that FBI special agents and other law enforcement officers are nervous about doing their work? They don't want to get sued, and they have no confidence that their agency would back them up 100 percent if they stood accused, such as in a lawsuit of this kind. Lawsuits are messy and mean lost money and lost time. No federal agency wants to invite lawsuits, so they pile on the warnings about what their employees can and cannot do.

This overreaction to potential lawsuits creates an atmosphere of fear, and sooner or later employees pull back instead of pushing ahead when their instincts and common sense tells them there is a major issue that should be investigated. Most federal agencies have become adverse to lawsuits to the degree that they are willing to overlook quite a bit just to avoid them.

This is where political courage comes in. The average FBI Special Agents need to concentrate on the mission and not allow PC to distract them from what they are supposed to be doing. They must be reminded by the management that the mission of the average FBI agent is *not* to avoid lawsuits at all costs, but to address the true *mission:* heading off more terrorist attacks against our nation.

And the White House and Congress can do their part by making it perfectly clear that they reject PC in all its forms and will fend off each and every frivolous lawsuit that the ACLU or anybody else might throw at them. If they need to hire more lawyers to do this, then bring them on board!

Yes, lawsuits take up a lot of time and cost the U.S. government lots of money, but consider what another terrorist attack will do to this nation's economy. Consider what the last one did to our federal budget! What costs more: the avoidance of lawsuits so as to adhere to the PC Police and the ACLU's wishes, or, dealing with the potential for lawsuits so we can avoid another terrorist attack?

To many, there is no choice; we must fight terrorism at the risk of offending some people. But the PC Police are very strong, and some claim they have a great deal of influence in the mainstream media. I know they have had a profound negative impact on the FBI.

Again, this is when a little political courage, the other PC, can save the day.

The other issue that needs to be addressed is the reflexive way the FBI managers handle whistleblowers and the bad news that they often bring.

# Let's Begin with FBI Headquarters

FBI Headquarters' Supervisory Special Agent (SSA) David Frasca's name has been leaked by concerned U.S. senators who *swear* everything they do is in the interest of the betterment of the FBI. Frasca was one of the managers at FBI Headquarters who Minneapolis FBI Agent and Legal Advisor Coleen Rowley named in her 13-page letter to FBI Director Robert Mueller, when questions began to swirl around the FBI after the attack.

Rowley also sent copies of her letter to several senators, so we'll assume she feared that the FBI Director would never see it. Was Rowley worried that the slugs below the director's 7th floor suite would make her bad news go away?

Who could have ever imagined what happened on September 11, 2001? But that doesn't relieve the responsibility of the FBI to respond to threats. Something bad happened at FBI Headquarters, and we have yet to learn what, or who is responsible. It's too easy to assume that David Frasca is to blame just because Rowley didn't leave any doubt in her memo about who she thinks obstructed the Phoenix and Minneapolis investigations.

But, is it as simple as Rowley claims? Is it true that SSA Frasca was in over his head and could not properly function in his job at FBI Headquarters for reasons related to a poor work ethic or abilities? I'm joining the chorus of people who insist—for our own future national security—that we learn what *really* happened at FBI Headquarters and how this important terrorist threat inquiry was stifled.

To start with, let's list the number of supervisory positions who could second-guess SSA Frasca.

• In Minneapolis, SSA Frasca interfaced with the field office supervisor who managed the squad that conducted the Moussaoui investigation.

• Immediately above the squad supervisor was an Assistant Special Agent in Charge (ASAC).

• Above him, there was a Special Agent in Charge (SAC) at the Minneapolis office.

All three of these individuals, or their acting counterparts could have weighed in on the Moussaoui investigation if they objected to

FBI Headquarters' decisions or inaction. Did they object? If Rowley's complaints were well-founded, we could assume the case agent, his supervisor, and Rowley went through the proper chain of command and complained to the ASAC and SAC. Rowley's memo does not seem to address this, but I think we need to know the answer.

At FBI Headquarters, above SSA Frasca is an Assistant Unit Chief. Above *his* assistant is the Unit Chief, who reports to the Assistant Section Chief. The Assistant Section Chief reports to the Assistant Director for the Division, and he reports to…you get the point.

Maybe what we really have here are plenty of chiefs, but not enough braves.

Many believe there are too many layers of management at the FBI overseeing the jobs of the street agents who do the real work. Recall the road repair crew with one guy digging in the hole with his pick, and five guys standing around the hole watching him dig. When we drive by this kind of bureaucratic waste, we often laugh. But if it happens at someplace important like the FBI, it isn't funny.

Then there's the typical knee-jerk reactions by Headquarters' denizens overly concerned with career advancement. Many are terrorized into timidity by the stories of others who came before—they tried to be proactive by helping field offices, but broke their pick off in the process. On more than one occasion SSAs have remarked, "No good deed goes unpunished." They aren't kidding, and that's sad. The best advice at FBI Headquarters is usually, "Keep your head down, your mouth shut, and just do your time."

"To get ahead, you have to get along; and to get along, you have to go along." I first heard this from my supervisor when I was a fresh recruit to the Washington Field Office SPIN Squad, the group responsible for conducting investigations of White House appointments. We handled Supreme Court Justice cases as well as investigations into the lives of the president's closest White House staff, including the Chief of Staff. It seemed very odd to me that FBI managers could adopt such dysfunctional attitudes, particularly with those involved in White House matters.

I too often heard, "The trouble with you, Aldrich, is that you care too much." Well, perhaps too many FBI managers don't care enough.

Director Mueller has a tough job ahead of him. He has proposed many changes, but the most important change may be the hardest one to make: the new FBI Director has promised a positive change in FBI management attitude, starting at the top.

The FBI needs this change desperately, and many of my friends, whether still in the FBI or retired from the bureau, suggest moving vast numbers of burned-out managers to the field offices for a fresh start, and bringing fresh managers from the field offices to headquarters, and many of these are ones who did not join the FBI so that they could go along to get along.

## More FBI Whistle Blowers Could Help

I was asked the other day by a television news show host working on a "fair and balanced network" if there was some way to find out what happened at the FBI that allowed al-Qaeda terrorists to attack us without "pointing the finger."

When it comes to demanding accountability for past failures on the part of elected and appointed government officials, what, may I ask, is wrong with pointing the finger?

I've pondered the host's question, and I've concluded that pointing the finger is a code phrase related to its first cousin, being judgmental. Heaven forbid that any of us are ever judgmental—we may actually hold someone accountable, forcing them to take responsibility for their actions.

Let's take a look at the congressional investigation concerning the September 11, 2001, terrorist attack. It continued for days, eventually featuring former FBI Director Louis Freeh. Freeh spent hours telling Congress why he believed the attacks of September 11 could not have been stopped. Of course we couldn't know precisely what would happen unless we had an informant working inside the group of hijackers. But we could not have an informant inside because over the years, Hard-Left Liberals have made sure the FBI and the CIA could not operate informants who came from questionable backgrounds.

So I agree with former FBI Director Freeh that the FBI and CIA cannot be held responsible for that. But can't these agency chiefs be held responsible for simply rolling over while Hard-Left politicians destroyed both agencies' abilities to protect national security?

The hand-wringers will whine, "But Aldrich, what did you expect them to do?" as they rush to protect the bureaucrats and ideological dunderheads on the Hard-Left. "Did you expect them to quit? Did you expect them to go public and complain to the media that misguided politicians were strangling their ability to protect a nation?"

Did you want these directors to become whistleblowers?! (gasp)

Yes! Exactly! I have said it before and will say it again: Men and women *of principle* will stand up and come forward, even at the risk of losing their jobs, if they have been asked to participate in something such as the dismantling of our nation's safeguards.

It's not as if Louis Freeh was unfamiliar with the concept of changing jobs. He had been an FBI agent, and then an FBI supervisor. He then became an Assistant U.S. Attorney. Later, he went into private practice, and then became a federal judge, appointed by President Bush 41.

So what did Director Freeh hope to accomplish by remaining in place while a corrupt president violated the law, misdirected the activities of the Department of Justice, apparently lied under oath and involved himself in obstruction of justice, and finally pardoned known foreign terrorists who had previously blown up New York City police officers?

Did Louis Freeh need his job that badly? By contrast, his resignation, coming at an appropriate time, could have focused a nation on the very real dangers facing us. But, Director Freeh stayed on, which did nothing but lull a nervous citizenry and Congress into believing that things were not that bad.

But things were that bad, and as the total picture develops, we find that things were much worse. And who would know the sorry state of our national security better than Louis Freeh? Well, perhaps the current CIA director, who also appears to need his present employment very badly.

FBI Director Freeh and CIA Director Tenet knew that their agencies could not communicate with each other—again the fault of their superiors. You see, Bill Clinton signed an executive order which made it impossible for the two agencies to trade important intelligence information if there was any chance that the trading of information could harm a future prosecution. As one FBI agent recently put it, "If Pearl Harbor was bombed today, I suppose they would tell us to go arrest the Emperor of Japan!"

One glaring failure for which Freeh is willing to admit responsibility is the dismal condition of the information management and dissemination system plaguing the FBI, a handicap that worsened as technology advanced. The antiques the FBI called computers were so old they could not even have been given away to trade schools as a donation!

But there is little evidence that Louis Freeh was aware of this. Insider sources tell me that Director Freeh rarely used the computer that stood in his own office. But this is not surprising, considering Freeh's previous employment as a federal judge when he had a staff of perhaps a dozen. All of those staff members understood that whatever a federal judge asks for, he gets. Freeh would not have needed to lift a finger to do anything for himself. He had a compliant staff to do it all!

Word processing? Forget about it! His secretary did that. Keeping track of evidence? Forget about it! He had legions of lawyers and clerks to file everything away and find it in a heartbeat. Phone numbers and addresses? There was somebody to do that, too. Freeh would have had no use for a computer.

There is no evidence available that he understood the capabilities that state-of-the-art computers had in identifying and tracking foreign terrorists, so how could he possibly have known how badly the FBI needed new computers? Bottom line: the FBI didn't get the needed computers, or the training to use them.

We used to hold people accountable, and we used to have men of character who would actually hold *themselves* accountable.

Of course there are numerous individuals who will be willing to line up behind Director Freeh and try to absolve him of responsibility. In what can only be described as an all-out assault on the homeland defense policies of the Bush administration, recently, the *Washington Post* published highly critical comments of six former top-level FBI officials. The criticism, which was also directed against the current leadership of the FBI, was led by none other than former FBI Director William H. Webster.

The policies under attack included the Justice Department's lengthy detention of known or suspected members of Osama bin Laden's terrorist network. The *Post's* front-page article was written by Jim McGee, a journalist described by former FBI agents as "an extremely liberal, left-leaning" fellow, formerly of the *Miami Herald*—the newspaper that has endorsed "terrorist experts" such as Bill Clinton, Al Gore and Janet Reno.

Some former FBI agents have expressed their belief to me that McGee sandbagged the ex-officials into making embarrassing comments that he could weave into a screed about the failure of the Department of Justice to properly care for the rights of illegal alien terrorists. This newest cause which revolves around so-called rights of non-citizens—even ones engaged in horrific acts of terrorism—seems to be gaining momentum among the usual civil-rights groups, other left-leaning groups, and the mainstream media.

However, McGee added a remarkable new spin by using his interviewees to suggest that the terrorists might be more valuable to the investigation if set free! Of course, no former FBI agents were interviewed who were willing to explain the absence of new terrorist acts since the roundup of hundreds of suspects. The fact that these hundreds are now unable to follow through on any plans they may have had to further terrorize this nation seems to escape the notice of our enterprising reporter.

One former official, scoffing at FBI plans to methodically interview thousands of witnesses, made no effort to hide his disdain for a related homeland defense policy. Former Assistant Director Kenneth P. Walton was quoted by McGee as stating, "It's the Perry Mason School of Law Enforcement, where you get them in there and they confess."

Walton ridiculed the plan to interview 5,000 Middle Eastern men: "Well, it just doesn't work that way. It is ridiculous. You say, 'Tell me everything you know,' and they give you the recipe to Mom's chicken soup."

When I think of all the time I wasted, trying to interview suspects...

The six former officials had all been involved in prevention of terrorism. Remarkably, William H. Webster, who had served as CIA director under both Presidents Reagan and Bush, was a paid lobbyist for airline industry interests and central to the defeat of proposed congressional legislation that would have forced airlines to tighten up airport security. Appearing before committees in 1998, Mr. Webster was asked if he would still favor lightened airport security if he was the current FBI or CIA chief. According to sources, Mr. Webster dodged the question by stating that the accuser was trying to compare apples and oranges.

With the FBI now stretched to its limits because of an unprecedented focus on two fronts—bombings and bio-terrorism—is it a wise idea to spring hundreds free, scattering them to the four winds to do whatever it is they want to do to us? Would you as a citizen interested in protecting your family be more confident or less confident of your safety with these suspected terrorists out of jail?

If the FBI promises to follow them closely so that they cannot escape to wreak their planned havoc on all of us, is that promise good enough for you? I think the FBI is darn good—but is the FBI that good? I think we'd be better off keeping terrorists locked up, but elements of the Hard-Left can always think of some reason why they should go free.

## What About Spies inside the FBI?

In 1964, President Lyndon B. Johnson's Chief of Staff, Walter Jenkins, was arrested in a public men's bathroom while engaged in a sexual liaison with a total stranger. It was not his first arrest. President Johnson demanded to know if there were others working in his White House who might embarrass the administration by infamous or outrageous conduct.

When President Johnson sought to reassure a nervous public that he had quality people working in his White House, he turned to the agency that had established the gold standard in personnel screening. He asked J. Edgar Hoover, FBI director, to send FBI Special Agents over to help screen White House employees.

Jenkins was no spy. His conduct, while troublesome and shameful, was not devastating to national security, but it could have been if hostile agents of a foreign government learned of his weakness for seeking sex with other men in public bathrooms. Such odd sexual behavior will always serve as a tool to blackmail a high-level White House official who would, understandably, want to keep such grotesque activities secret.

The nation's mind was set at ease after the FBI's system of personnel screening was adopted, and for 30 years, until the arrival of Bill Clinton, the security system at the White House fulfilled its mission.

Unknown to the White House, or apparently any oversight committee tasked with watching agencies like the FBI, a steady erosion of the FBI's own personnel screening and security system was well underway. Evidently, nobody was watching the watchers.

In 1993, when FBI street agents like me tried to get the attention of FBI managers about the breakdown of security procedures at the Clinton White House, we were soundly rebuffed. I was puzzled as to why FBI managers at the field office level and at FBI Headquarters were not more concerned. After all, the FBI has a responsibility to protect national security—it's one of its primary missions.

In addition, as the lead agency in the screening of all the President's high-level cabinet appointees, federal judges, including Supreme Court Justices and members of boards assembled to investigate and access the nation's most important work—requiring high-level security clearances—the FBI was a full partner, not just a concerned bystander, in the process of screening White House employees.

But the FBI was never an enthusiastic partner with the Secret Service and the White House Counsel's office in this very important work. People in the FBI made no effort to conceal their hatred and disgust for screening positions. Now we know, because of the recently released Webster Report, that FBI management had little interest in finding and removing troubled employees from its own ranks.

I was well aware of the poor attitudes expressed by the average FBI manager relative to the dreaded applicant work. Agents who were sent to applicant assignments were considered victims of a cruel fate, or lesser agents, or were suspected of poor performance. Ironically, thoughtless or clueless top-level FBI managers would often use applicant squads as dumping grounds for misbehaving agents. It was well known that personnel security received no respect.

Of course, those who took personnel screening seriously strongly objected. But upper management ignored our concerns. If we persisted, complaining that we didn't want the office's problem agents dumped on us, we would be punished for rocking the boat.

This remarkable attitude, so terribly destructive to the quality of the FBI's own working force, was a direct result of high-level FBI management attitudes. Once, attending a reception at FBI Headquarters for a manager who had finally escaped the applicant units for more worthwhile work, the FBI assistant director turned to me and said, "Aldrich, when are you going to get wise and get out of this applicant business? Only somebody remarkably stupid would try to stay in this miserable line of work."

But FBI agents like me who chose to take these assignments saw benefits others could not see. For example, I would no longer be forced to deal with lousy and dishonest defense attorneys, arrogant federal judges and endless waves of criminals and their victims. I'd had a 20-year career of that, and although I was good at it, I was tired of it.

I also joined those who had an understanding of the importance of screening presidential appointments. Working at the White House was an assignment that offered a chance to finish my career around semi-normal people! I mean, how normal are politicians? At least they were more normal than the folks I previously associated with!

That is, until Bill Clinton and his gang came to town.

Nevertheless, FBI agents like me were greeted with suspicion by agents who believed kicking in doors and arresting felons was the only worthwhile work of an FBI agent.

My partner at the White House was an accomplished FBI agent in his own right and a Vietnam Veteran. It was his lifelong dream to catch a real spy, and that is why he wanted to work at the White House. He wanted to be the first FBI agent to catch a spy working for a president.

Apparently, I was one of a very few at the FBI who thought that was a great idea.

How sad that my partner's dream was not appreciated by FBI managers. They could have used a dozen like him over at FBI Headquarters. Maybe he, who also was made to suffer for taking his job so seriously, would have caught Robert Hanssen.

The FBI can follow all the investigative hearings and commission recommendations, establish new rules, pass new laws and warn agents daily, but until FBI management is forced to change their awful attitude about applicant work, they won't prevent another Robert Hanssen.

# FBI Turf War is Way Overblown

One sure way for politicians to avoid responsibility is to cause subordinate agencies to get involved in a finger-pointing contest. After September 11, 2001, there have been many media accounts of an alleged turf war between the FBI and certain local law enforcement agencies that some claim may hamper the FBI's ability to solve our terrorist problems.

Having walked a 26-year mile in the shoes of an FBI agent, I can relate to the real concerns they have about sharing too much information with the locals.

The differences between the federals and the locals are vast. First, one key difference is that every FBI agent has been through an extensive background investigation and was granted a top secret clearance before assuming official duties. Access to U.S. government secrets is not only a necessity, but also holds tremendous legal implications. We cannot ask the FBI to simply waive federal law, even in the face of this most horrific threat. But if Congress and the Executive Branch want to do this, they have the power—the FBI does not.

Secondly, you cannot have a blanket policy to share highly confidential information with the locals. Despite the fact that the United States has had a decade-long national policy of local law enforcement enhancements in education and salary benefits to ensure high quality officers and leadership, it's a sad fact that in too many police departments the incompetence still runs wide and deep.

Nevertheless, in most major cities with good departments, the FBI has already set up task forces to work hand-in-hand with the locals. In my years of service I have worked with local and state officers in several jurisdictions, and these fine officers had background investigations, clearances, and access to FBI office space on a daily basis. So, to make a claim that the FBI is not working with locals is bogus. Any cooperation is carefully thought out so that the investigation—and national security—is protected.

Consider that when the FBI shuns the locals' offers of help and mutual cooperation, there may be good reason. Yes, it's true that the locals have more officers and usually have a better grasp of who's in the neighborhood. They may even know who might be a terrorist or a terrorist sympathizer, but how would the FBI ever control thousands of local police officers if they were all briefed with the best information known only to the FBI?

The fact is they could not.

Moreover, if a local police officer or police chief has important information to give to the FBI, it would be incomprehensible for them to refuse to reveal the information because of some perceived snit that a local police chief or politician thinks he is having with the feds. So, we'll assume that the local police chiefs can order their officers to turn over every rock to find these terrorist swine.

The FBI, to my knowledge, has not asked any locals to back off on their investigations, and even if they did, I am not sure the FBI has the power to stop a local investigation. Only a U.S. attorney can do that.

It's one thing to give key information to somebody you know and trust. It's quite another thing to trust that your most important case is safe in the hands of a stranger—badge or no badge. I would suggest that the current criticism of the FBI—even if printed in the editorial pages of the mighty *Washington Post*—is gratuitous. There are appropriate times to criticize our nation's premier law enforcement agency (everybody knows I am not blindly loyal to my former employer), but I know the difference between honest, constructive criticism and reflexive bashing.

I fear the average citizen cannot tell the difference, and I know that our enemies and the conspiracy wing nuts are rubbing their hands together in glee at this latest unfair attack on the FBI. Cooler heads will resist a temptation of piling on an agency that has its hands full right now, helping to save our skins.

Regardless of the scope of local/federal cooperation, the FBI is the agency that will get the blame if something about the investigation goes sour. Consider what happened in Atlanta during the 1996 summer Olympics: a bomb killed and maimed citizens after someone left a backpack bomb in a public square. The Clinton administration ordered a joint task-force to investigate this horrible crime, and the FBI was ordered to work with state and local officers, as well as many federal agencies, including the ATF.

Within a very short time, a suspect was developed and the FBI turned its laser focus in Richard Jewell's direction. Almost immediately, the national news media received a tip that Jewell could be the bomber, and their collective attention turned Jewell's life into a living nightmare.

Richard Jewell's reputation was ruined, and no matter how much time goes by, the Atlanta bombing can never be mentioned without including Richard Jewell's name in the same breath.

Did the FBI leak Jewell's identity to the news media? There is not a shred of evidence that the FBI was responsible for this leak, and it is well known that there were hundreds of local, state and federal law enforcement officers involved in the investigation, not to mention dozens of prosecutors and quite a few politicians as well. Regardless, the FBI got the blame for this very damaging leak and will forever be held responsible for ruining Richard Jewell's life.

Is it possible that certain key FBI managers fear that the same thing can, and probably will, happen again? This current case is the most important case the FBI has ever investigated and has real potential for allowing the FBI to regain much lost credibility and popularity. By the same token, it has the obvious potential of ruining the agency's reputation for all time if things go seriously wrong.

Those who watch he FBI closely agree—the agency cannot afford another misstep.


## FBI and NASA's Problems Similar

In 1986, while having lunch with a former FBI agent and good friend who had gone on to work in NASA's Inspector General's office, he and I watched in horror as the space shuttle Challenger blew up into millions of pieces. We stared open-mouthed as the dying crew and flaming debris spiraled down from the sky.

On February 1, 2003, my children and I watched as another space shuttle and crew was horribly destroyed. It will take a long time for the investigative commission to issue a report, but we do know what happened the last time a shuttle blew up.

NASA's reputation disintegrated following the Challenger explosion as revelations from whistleblowers confirmed the worst fears: a simple rubber O-Ring failure that caused the Challenger accident could have been prevented if only certain NASA careerists had not been so paralyzed by their long-standing bureaucratic attitudes.

A forced outside examination of NASA's accident resulted in a sweeping management shake up. Until February 1, NASA had not experienced another accident or loss of life. A sense of optimism, confidence and excellence had been restored to NASA's mission.

There are similarities between NASA and the FBI, but whereas NASA was forced to undergo a complete management overhaul, the FBI hasn't been forced to fix its own O-Ring problems.

Both agencies have critical missions that remain close to the hearts of Americans. NASA and the FBI, by way of their action or inaction, have the power over life and death. Rocket science is very dangerous, without question. If it were not for the constant vigilance of every NASA employee, more lives would surely be lost in our quest to explore the heavens.

Likewise, the FBI conducts high-risk investigations at times requiring agents to use and dodge lethal firepower.

Most would agree that both agencies' missions capture the public's imagination due to the life-altering and life-threatening context of their work. Movies, books, and television have explored and capitalized on the fascination we have for the dangers that NASA and the FBI face daily.

The limited vacancies that occur in each agency are highly sought after, and a large percentage of employees stay until retirement age. Careers in aerospace and law enforcement, no doubt, require mature, intelligent and educated employees who can pass through exhaustive background investigations enabling access to top-secret material. The American people have a right to expect that anyone hired by NASA or the FBI must command respect and act in the best interests of the nation as they seek to achieve their mission. After all, they are public employees. They are well paid and receive tremendous benefits like generous retirement and health care packages that most citizens can only dream of.

Americans need their heroes, and they are used to finding them in the cockpits of the space shuttles, at the firing ranges and in the good news headlines about the work of the FBI. Americans don't want bad news and they're willing to pay plenty of hard-earned tax dollars to get what they want.

NASA and the FBI favor former military experience because there is a tremendous need for discipline and a no-nonsense approach to the agencies mission objectives. Following orders is essential. Predictably, mavericks or boat-rockers are deemed to be troublesome, worthy of shunning by management and other employees. Most FBI and NASA personnel are a patriotic lot as well, possessing a team spirit that helps them achieve their missions.

There is also a sense of a special calling. For example, quite a few of the FBI agents I worked with had studied for the ministry or considered other vocations that required commitments beyond the usual employment experience. My friends in NASA have confirmed that they see the same kind of dedication there: long hours, high risk, high stress, and totally focused dedication, oftentimes at the expense of family relationships.

These are qualities that can be found in both agencies.

NASA's recent shortcomings, if any, are yet to be discovered. What's wrong with the FBI is well known: There's a significant management problem at FBI Headquarters. Attorney General John Ashcroft is correct to assume that one way to fix the management problem is through the use of outside industry management experts who can clearly see what too many myopic middle and upper-level FBI managers choose to ignore.

Herein lies one difference between NASA and the FBI: NASA managers seemed embarrassed and frightened by their own incompetence and selfish devotion to careerism, but there has been no sign that FBI managers are ready to concede anything other than the existence of some Left or Right Wing Conspiracy with media accomplices dedicated to dragging the FBI down.

Inside the FBI, no criticism is considered fair no matter how honest, no matter how well intentioned. The attitude that I describe here is the posture of the beleaguered, the defensiveness of the cornered. For the FBI's own good, and the good of the nation, there needs to be radical reform at the FBI, whether bureaucratic careerists at the agency like it or not!

Their willingness to embrace or oppose change is irrelevant. These men and women who carry guns and can seize liberty and property must possess the attitudes of 747 pilots not the mentality of the chased and trapped.

American citizens care deeply about the FBI and NASA. We, as a nation, must demand the strictest adherence to quality and performance standards. We should expect nothing less from the men and women who give us carefree streets in which to roam.

## Closing Thoughts about the FBI

With the second anniversary of our nation's most devastating terrorist attack a mere six months away, we cannot help but reevaluate the progress of our FBI. We continue to ask the question of whether the new FBI director can straighten out the obvious management problems and the political correctness that have vexed the nation's most important federal law enforcement agency.

The answer is given on a daily basis as we realize we've had no catastrophic terrorist attack since September 11, 2001. In the days following, FBI Director Mueller spent much time meeting with the president. My sources tell me that at one meeting as Mueller was trying to recite facts about the terrorist attack—to illustrate the FBI's ability to conduct a post-crime investigation—the president made it clear that he was less interested in finding out what happened, and more interested in preventing future attacks.

During the course of a single conversation, George W. Bush defined the problem facing the FBI and fixed it. With his new marching orders, Director Muller returned to the FBI and began a policy overhaul that has resulted in the departure of many of the FBI's senior management. The sweeping personnel changes at 9th and Pennsylvania have echoes in the FBI's field offices as well, because vacancies and policy changes at the top cause a major reshuffling out in the field.

Those senior managers who could not get with the new program, or who stood guilty of foot-dragging on important terrorism leads from the field, such as those developed in Minneapolis and Phoenix, found themselves transferred, demoted, or the subjects of severe arm-twisting to elicit retirement papers. When you look at FBI Headquarters today, there are fewer senior managers who served under the previous FBI Director, Louis Freeh.

To understand the significant change in the approach to the investigation of terrorism by the FBI, one needs only to look back at the eight years of Bill Clinton's administration. Recall that all attacks against the interest of this nation were treated as crimes requiring high-profile investigations, and the FBI was the lead agency given the case.

Thus, when embassies were bombed by Osama bin Laden, Clinton called on the FBI to conduct a criminal investigation instead of ordering a military strike. When suicide bombers in an inflatable boat blew out the side of a U.S. warship in Yemen, acting on orders by bin Laden, again Clinton ordered the FBI to conduct a criminal investigation.

There were many other examples of how the FBI was used by the Clinton-Reno-Freeh team to address international terrorism in this less lethal way, but the important thing to note here is that the FBI's internal resources were not being well utilized. In fact, FBI assets were being squandered by an administration determined to side-step the bin Laden problem—a growing menace with proven ability and plainly stated objectives: to kill Jews and Americans.

Before September 11, the FBI was basically divided into two parts. On one side was the criminal division which had the responsibility for making sure federal laws were being enforced. On the other side of the FBI were the spooks, working on foreign counter intelligence and domestic terrorism. The difficultly in merging the two functions is obvious: when you chase foreign spies you use sensitive methods and means to get the information you need to access the threat and hopefully neutralize the dangers. This includes lots of electronic eavesdropping and other techniques that the FBI and other intelligence agencies don't want exposed in some criminal case discovery proceeding.

The FBI does not do this clandestine work alone. The CIA, NSA, Department of Defense and the Secret Service—as well as intelligence agencies of foreign allies—all work together against world terrorism or dangerous political "isms" including those that currently strangle the citizens of Cuba, China and North Korea.

Consider the inherent dangers that a criminal case creates for the deeply placed agents who secretly serve the U.S. in foreign lands. Federal judges can often order the federal government to produce witnesses for the defense, even if they are highly placed spies. One criminal case can wipe out dozens of sensitive eyes and ears as well as disclose the federal government's more secretive intelligence gathering technology.

In other words, the FBI divisions were not only fighting for turf and budget, not to mention face-time with the director, but were fighting to maintain a wall between their respective divisions so that both could operate effectively. In this struggle, the criminal division had much to gain, and the counter intelligence division had much to lose.

The Clinton administration preferred the clumsy, ineffective path of trying to bring terrorists to court—a path that could result in catastrophic destruction for U.S. interests, and did. But a criminal case, by its very ponderous nature, bought time for Bill Clinton and his failed foreign policy. One day Bill Clinton was no longer president, then somebody else was left holding the tab for an eight-year-long party during which time Clinton was able to avoid making hard choices, such as going to war with Osama bin Laden.

The strike against us on September 11 has given our new president an opportunity to reshape an agency badly in need of reform. Mere management shake-ups and reorganization would not have accomplished much, no matter how well intended, planned or executed. There was an entrenched mentality of how things should be done in the senior ranks of the FBI. Eight years of Bill Clinton and nearly eight years of Louis Freeh, reinforced that mentality.

The FBI has a new mission: to head off terrorism, to prevent future attacks. This means that much of what the FBI does and learns will never see the light of day. The new mission greatly empowers the intelligence side of the agency and helps to streamline the criminal side. No longer will the FBI be able to afford taking on every Tom, Dick, and Harry violation of federal law that a pandering congress wants to throw at it.

A leaner, meaner FBI is being crafted as I write. The inherent danger of this newly shaped agency is that future politicians may be able to use the FBI to investigate domestic dissent, claiming that any opposition to the federal government's agendas may indicate a willingness to commit terrorist acts.

History gives us a few examples to support this: abortion clinics blown up by pro-life advocates on the Right, various citizens blown up with letter bombs from a nutcase on the Hard-Left, and, of course, the bombing of the Oklahoma Federal Office Building, all serve as rationalization for some to watch our own citizens more closely.

But do these cases justify increased citizen scrutiny? Such domestic terrorist acts are rare, and when closely examined, it's easily determined that these terrorists—deranged criminals, really—have mostly acted on their own.

Will the FBI end up investigating us all by claiming that every one of us has potential to be a future terrorist because we have an opinion different from the party in power? These are the questions that we should be asking the FBI today.

The pratfalls of the FBI's past are becoming a distant memory in the wake of September 11. Let's hope we've seen the last of these significant and preventable errors. But can we get security from terrorists—domestic or foreign—without significant loss of civil liberties?

To prevent such a loss requires close scrutiny of the FBI's practices. Let's make sure they're investigating the right people and not looking into your business or mine because we happen to own a gun or vocally support a politician who adores the Bible or the Bill of Rights.

# CHAPTER EIGHT—
# Every Citizen a Soldier

The recent sniper killings in the D.C. area only provide more evidence that there can never be enough government enforcement officers to protect us all. That means we must be ready to protect ourselves.

By arming ourselves we have a chance to save our lives or the lives of the ones we love. We might even be able to save an innocent third party, if circumstances arise. And, one by-product of exercising our fundamental rights of self-protection and gun ownership is the very real deterrent those arms represent to those who would try to take away our liberty.

Advocates for the reach and growth of government, in terms of agendas and personnel, have worked hard to create a myth that bigger is better. Such mythology is expensive and dangerous because it lulls us into thinking we no longer have to hone skills of self-reliance and self-defense.

Notions of an omnipotent government create a fiction that as long as citizens are willing to pay more taxes, they can expect that they'll be required to do little else but vote and perhaps serve on a jury once in a while.

Our form of government works best if every adult citizen participates. But lately, it seems that citizens are being discouraged from becoming witnesses.

The message we hear from government leaders involved in the recent D.C. area shootings is that witnesses are too stupid to know what they've just seen. There are just too many derisive comments by police authorities claiming that eyewitness accounts are "notoriously inaccurate." If what they say is believed, will we soon see the end of witnesses at trials, except for those experts who are "pre-qualified" to observe?

And since when is making negative comments about witnesses helpful to the eventual successful prosecution of a case?

Even a Republican administration contributes to a widening gulf between ordinary citizens and the elites of our day by promoting a TIPS program in connection with the War on Terrorism. TIPS stands for Terrorist Information and Prevention System. The theory goes that only some of us, pre-approved by the federal government, will be asked to be on the lookout for terrorists.

The rest of us are drones, I guess.

With a "don't try this at home—it's too dangerous" attitude on the part of the government, how soon will it be before average citizens who actually see something important will be reluctant to come forward for fear some government authority will treat their evidence with disrespect or outright derision?

Since when do we give a pass to citizens by implying that they need not do anything at all, even if they see important terrorist or criminal activity? What kind of message are we sending to our children with this elitist approach? Mind your own business?

Crime and terrorism are *everyone's* business!

How things have changed in these United States. We used to all pull together during dangerous times. Today, the government finds ways to sort us into groups consisting of those who are authorized to see something versus those who can't be trusted with what they see with their own eyes.

But when a million eyes and ears in the Washington area went on the alert for the various vehicles allegedly used by the shooters, these killers were found and arrested quickly.

Who found them? Why, ordinary citizens, that's who!

It took longer to arrest these killers because they were black. One was an angry Black Muslim. But, the authorities had been convinced that the killer(s) had to be an angry white male, perhaps a former military sniper.

All leads pointing to two black men were dismissed immediately. These two apparently homeless guys driving a suspicious vehicle with out of state tags at odd hours were seen over the course of many days, often near the scene of one of the shootings—but they were not interrogated because they were black!

Can't we make a case that political correctness has become dangerous, and is actually killing more and more of us each day?

The Hard-Left rants about killer SUVs, and yet when a major snow storm hit the Washington, D.C., area, calls went out from hospitals and emergency care facilities for SUVs to transport doctors, nurses and patients to and from the hospital.

Except, it was politically *in*correct to call them SUVs, so they were called 4-wheel drive vehicles instead. I'm sure the patients needing medical care, and the new mother ready to deliver, were thrilled to see that SUV coming down the road.

Isn't it ironic that a society that prides itself on higher education, increased SAT scores, and informed citizens is the same society which is led by government officials who do not consider the citizens smart enough to witness and accurately report a crime?

How is it that as we become smarter, the government thinks we're less intelligent?

Maybe it's just evidence of the arrogance of power.

One obvious way government authorities treat citizens like children is their endless attempt to disarm the population. This effort goes on in spite of the clear wording in the Constitution that guarantees our right to "keep and bear arms." In states like Virginia, violent crime continues to go down while citizens avail themselves with concealed-carry permits that the state must issue whenever shown proof of the required training.

That makes every man and every woman a potential member of a modern-day posse. There is evidence that more and more people are becoming wise to claims that the government knows how to do almost everything better than you can. By definition, only you can provide *self-defense.*

Recently, The Patrick Henry Center, an organization that I founded, has trained nearly a hundred women, empowering them to carry firearms, perhaps concealed in their belts or purses. These newly energized and equipped citizens are not only exercising their rights, but they are also experiencing a new-found freedom—freedom from the constant fear of attack by violent predators.

For years, the government (and our friends at NOW, etc.) have been telling women that personnel and tons of money will keep them safe. This is not necessarily a bold-faced lie, but neither is it the truth. People still have to do some things for themselves if they want to have the best chance of avoiding becoming a victim.

Admittedly, there is little we can do to stop a sniper who stealthily sneaks up on his victim and fires that deadly shot. But might not a sniper be a bit more hesitant to commence such an operation if he knew he was surrounded by armed citizens?

That is, if we're not blinded by political correctness.

It defies common sense to suggest, as government officials do, that it is only they—or their approved representatives—who are qualified to search for D.C. area assassins, or anybody else, for that matter. Ignoring the millions of eyes and ears that could otherwise be available to help authorities may mean that killers and terrorists will get more time to do their deadly work.

People need to be encouraged to stop, look, and listen. They don't need to be told that their observations are nearly worthless to law enforcement. Every clue will be helpful in protecting ourselves and our families. Even if an overly-excited citizen gets some of it wrong, there is much more that he or she will get right!

All the clues put together will solve cases of killing and terror, and the sooner the better.

An obvious attitude is coming from those who claim that government can do anything for you if only you'll agree to give them more power and send in more money.

The truth is, most of the time the police are guessing just like the rest of us.

Police know from experience that there is a high probability that a mere citizen will provide the information that will enable them to make that arrest. Another good reason to encourage and praise citizens is that we are the very ones who are paying their salaries!

And, not incidentally, ordinary citizens are the ranks from which most of the dead and wounded have been taken—we have a stake in this process! So let's behave as if we're all in this together—because we are.

Self-reliance and self-defense may be alien concepts here in the bigger cities like D.C., but out in the Heartland folks remember how to protect themselves—and their methods don't include total reliance on arrogant bureaucracies whose spokespersons suggest, "Duck down if you hear a shot."

Government authorities should work together with ordinary citizens and combine the best qualities of both groups to stop the killing, and catch the terrorist scum.

## Living in Fear

Consider a real terrorist act that took place outside CIA headquarters a few years ago. The shooter met morning rush hour traffic turning into the CIA gates and systematically shot people as they waited in their cars to go through security. He was able to escape, but was later identified because of an excellent investigation conducted by several dedicated agencies, including the FBI. It was determined that he was a foreign terrorist—an America hater—and had selected the CIA headquarters because it was believed the killings would terrorize the CIA and the nation.

We would later learn that associates of Osama bin Laden were planning more carnage at the CIA by diving hijacked commercial airliners full of passengers into the many office buildings located there. On September 11, 2001, the targets turned out to be the Twin Towers and the Pentagon. But it's possible the CIA was once again a target—one hijacked plane was taken over by the passengers and later crashed in Pennsylvania. Moreover, after September 11, box cutters were found secreted in at least one other aircraft, so we'll never know if other hijackings were planned but thwarted by quick action from the Bush White House to ground all commercial aircraft.

Our violent history recalls one white-hating shooter aboard the Long Island Railroad, who for whatever reason, decided he had suffered enough discrimination at the hands of white people. He calmly walked through the railcars, shooting and reloading at will, until many were killed. Passengers were finally able to subdue this monster after he stopped to reload again.

Then there were the Son of Sam killings in New York City. An individual stalked the streets of New York, looking for lovers sitting in cars. When he found them, voices in his head would tell him to shoot. He killed several innocents until the police could put together enough facts to determine who the real killer was. He was not aligned with any political group, he was simply twisted, just like the two teenagers in Colorado who walked the halls of Columbine High School killing innocent students, especially those who had expressed a love for Christ.

The point is: the only thing standing between the average innocent citizen and a horrible death at the hands of a real terrorist or a nut is…nothing.

Absolutely nothing stops an organized killer working for a terrorist or a crazy person who is listening to voices in his or her head, unless a law enforcement officer stumbles upon the crime being committed. In a society with too few police officers and millions of freely roaming citizens, the odds of a killer being caught in the act are slim to none.

Maryland and the District of Columbia have some of the toughest gun laws in the country. These overlapping, and some say unconstitutional, gun laws have done nothing to make Maryland and D.C. safer. Layer upon layer of gun laws simply don't work.

Instead, the average law-abiding citizen can only watch in horror as a shooter aims and fires his weapon, then runs or drives away.

The unarmed citizen can write down a vehicle description and perhaps get a tag number. This is how most killers are eventually caught. Of course, most police cars are marked, so cunning predators can wait until a police car turns a corner. And, although there are many good undercover officers who can blend in and perhaps catch monsters as they lay in wait for the next victim, the number of uniformed police officers far outnumbers the undercover types.

You cannot have a cop on every corner. What part of this does the Hard-Left not understand?

All of the conventional statistics prove that when citizens have the right to arm themselves and carry concealed weapons, the crime rate goes down. The snipers set up camp in the unarmed state of Maryland. Could it be that they knew they had little to fear from the law-abiding citizens who are helpless against such armed killers?

If just one person had been armed on that train in Long Island, or if one school official had been armed at Columbine, could there have been a different outcome? As we know, two ordinary citizens finally caught the D.C. snipers. Thank God the snipers were sleeping, because the unarmed citizens probably would have been killed.

One thing is for certain: those who live in states that permit their law-abiding to carry concealed weapons are citizens who have less to fear from armed terrorists, whether foreign or domestic. Citizens of these states constitute a volunteer army of law enforcement officers, multiplying the number of possibilities of stopping madness before it starts.

## *The Hard-Left Never Lets Up*

The Hard-Left is coming after your guns. You see, if they can't get them, then they'll never move this country to Hard-Socialism—which is where they want to go with this twisted game of theirs. They have a lot of "useful idiots" to help them get there.

Consider that a professor of journalism at the University of Ohio was recently ordered to remove a Civil War relic from his office wall. Of course he protested because the university's policy is silly and unrealistic. Some school administrators and liberal professors were upset because he holds opinions different from their own, and they've found a way to get even with him. They've set out to get him, and sadly, it appears they have the power to do so.

Professor Patrick S. Washburn now awaits his rhetorical hanging—and perhaps the end of his professional career—simply because he's willing to stand up for his rights.

His great-grandfather's rifle, long ago rendered inoperable, is considered to be in violation of a workplace violence policy regarding weapons of any kind on campus, even those used for display. Someone who visited his office or heard about his rifle, lodged a complaint, and soon, armed campus police were at his door. They strongly suggested that he remove the display or face disciplinary actions, including possible dismissal from employment.

The professor, a practicing Conservative, was determined to exercise his rights to free expression by fighting back. Aware that the

Ohio University football team fired a small cannon at games to signal a touchdown, he suggested that this weapon—one that actually does work—should also be forbidden if campus policy was to be followed to the letter.

The cannon is fully operational, and while it's only used to explode harmless gunpowder, it could be loaded with nails or bolts and shot up into the crowd. By contrast, Professor Washburn's rifle, also used as a symbol, could never be fired.

What causes some otherwise rational people to go off the deep end with nonsensical policies that are obviously selectively enforced? Some suggest that recent school shootings have brought new attention to the age-old problem of violence, especially when it involves firearms on campus.

But, if they are really concerned about violence, how do gun control fundamentalists reconcile the fact that most major university campuses are rife with violent acts being committed against female students, but so little is done about it?

Put another way, do you have to die in order to get any attention from campus do-gooders?

Why do gun control fundamentalists passionately fight Conservatives who only want to protect their First and Second Amendment rights but find little time to make sure coeds are not raped or assaulted on campus? It's a sad and well-known fact that women make easy targets for sexual attacks by violent predators simply because they usually cannot protect themselves.

What does the average sexual predator know about college campuses? First, there is only a token police presence to protect those on campus. Second, everybody except the police is ordered to keep weapons of all kinds off campus. And third, the campus is amply stocked with hundreds, if not thousands, of attractive young females, each one a potential target for a violent sexual predator.

If you were a rapist, where would you go to select your next target? Willy Sutton, a well-known bank robber, was once asked why he robbed banks. "Because that's where the money is," replied Sutton, obviously amused that anybody would ask such a dumb question. What was not reported was that Sutton, as well as other violent criminals, always cased a potential target and stayed away from those situations where it was likely that victims could put up any fight!

There's been no evidence that Professor Washburn was violent. On the contrary, there's plenty of evidence that he's a caring individual concerned about the rights of others. He's hardworking and law-abiding. His real sin may only be that he attempted to practice his conservative values on a very liberal campus.

But Ohio University, in its wisdom, has decided that the mere appearance of a rifle, even an inoperable one owned by a normal, mature professional man with a good reputation, poses some threat to the university population.

It would be a refreshing change to find school administrators who think critically and logically when it comes to issues of self-protection for the young people parents entrust to their care.

How many students were shot last year with inoperable Civil War relics? On the other hand, how many female students were mugged, battered, robbed, or raped? How many of those innocent victims were allowed, or even encouraged, to defend themselves?

# Fundamental Truths

I recently spent the day with one of the founders of a group opposed to gun control, the Second Amendment Sisters (SAS). You may recall that on a recent Mother's Day there was the so-called Million Mom March, except that it was not a million moms as advertised. Instead, it was several thousand highly emotional, well-funded women who descended upon Washington, D.C., to demand that politicians pass more gun control laws.

Five brave women from around the country refused to buy into the flawed logic of the Moms. They could not allow a political interest group to claim that they spoke for the women of America. Juli Bednarzyk and four of her Internet friends believed there was a majority of women who were certain they had the right to defend themselves, including the use of firearms, if it came to that.

With a few dollars, Internet emails and web site networking (www.2asisters.org), SAS built momentum for a counter-march on Washington, D.C., that blunted the Mom's efforts and took away a lot of the media attention. Thousands of newly minted Second Amendment Sisters came to D.C., and with both points of view represented, it was impossible for the Mom's to claim they represented all women.

I asked Juli, a young professional with a demanding full-time career, what would possess her to leave her job, her family, her hometown of Chicago, and come to D.C. at her own expense to raise the argument for gun ownership. Juli stated that she and her friends believe that there are certain fundamental truths that as a society we can all agree upon.

One such truth is the slogan of SAS: Self Defense is a Basic Human Right.

As a former law enforcement officer who carried a concealed firearm on the job and off, I understood the wisdom of Juli's position. For 26 years I did my job then headed home to extend the protection my federal firearm granted me to my family, my friends, my neighborhood store—virtually everywhere I went. How beneficial to have that level of protection available to my family and myself, and even to total strangers if I witnessed a crime in progress.

What wonderful freedom from the fear ordinary citizens face day after day. But, if an off-duty federal agent and your average police officer can enjoy that level of protection, why is it that the average law-abiding citizen cannot?

The federal government has recently admitted that it can't possibly protect us from every threat. Some, like Juli, knew that was yet another fundamental truth. The irrefutable evidence was a smoldering rubble pile in New York City and a big hole in the Pentagon.

Even President Bush's Homeland Security Czar warned us that, "everyone should be an air marshal" when traveling the less-than-friendly skies. He knows the impossibility of having an armed air marshal on every flight.

Has the September 11, 2001, attack on our nation cleared the way for logical discussions about the right of every citizen to protect themselves against violence, no matter what form it may take? Recent press reports of a major increase in gun sales should come as no big surprise, but what's really interesting is that many of the gun purchasers are women, and many of these same women have applied for Right to Carry permits in the 33 states that allow citizens—not just cops—to defend themselves.

Patrick Henry has been considered the voice of the American Revolution, and when people remember what Henry is famous for, they usually refer to his *Liberty or Death* speech. But how many Americans know why he made that speech at St. John's Church in the first place? There he convinced the other leaders that war with the British was inevitable, and that a well-trained, well-equipped militia should be formed without delay.

But was this the first time colonists had considered the use of firearms for protection against violence? Hardly. The gun had been a tool used for self-defense and hunting long before the British became an issue, and history books prove that it was not only the men who knew how to use them. Women and young children were trained to load and fire the weapons because the men could not always be around to protect them against the beasts and savages that were part of every settler's reality.

Consider the following passage lifted right out of our Declaration of Independence: "He has excited domestic insurrections amongst us, and has endeavored to bring on the inhabitants of our frontiers, the merciless Indian Savages, whose known rule of warfare is an undistinguished destruction of all ages, sexes and conditions."

In other words, the terrorists of Henry's time also killed innocent civilians: the children, the women, the sick, and the elderly.

And who protected the children and the homesteads while the men were off fighting the British? Yet another fundamental truth emerges: our women were pressed into service, and by all accounts they did a splendid job—and not by calling 911 to seek a police officer who could not possibly ride fast enough to save them.

They swallowed hard, grabbed their guns, and did what they had to do.

In those days, nobody debated the political correctness of gun ownership. Slowly but surely, our society became frivolous to the degree that we actually began to believe that somehow the government could do everything for us...that is, until September 11.

But Juli Bednarzyk and her Second Amendment Sisters—and a lot of other Americans—always knew better than that.

# A Few Untapped Resources

I've flown a number of times since September 11, 2001, and I can truthfully admit that I was not very comfortable getting on an airplane when I knew that the lowest bidder had won the airline contract to screen passengers and secure the working areas of most of our nation's international airports.

Now that the federal government has taken over airport security, things are a lot better, but there are still a lot of holes in the system, and there will never be enough armed air marshals available for every flight.

As I sat in the waiting room, before my first flight after September 11, I watched my fellow passengers. I had promised my worried wife, also a former FBI agent, that I would do everything in my power to ensure my safe return.

As I scanned the crowd looking for odd people, violent looking people, or those who might match a terrorist profile, I suddenly realized I was back on the job!

Two federal marshals walked down the corridor and stopped in my area to do the same thing I was doing. They scanned the group. They were in uniform and were armed. I was younger than both, and I could tell from their appearance that I was more physically fit. I mention this only because the thought occurred to me that except for the gun, I had everything they had to protect my flight against a terrorist attack.

When I boarded the plane, I looked at each passenger and attempted to establish eye contact. Some people will not look up no matter what's going on because they don't want anyone to see their eyes. Often, they behave this way because they're shy. Sometimes they avoid eye contact because they are trying to hide something. It is against human nature to not look at the arriving passengers. Some are handsome and pretty, some unusual, but all humans are interesting to law enforcement officers—on the job or retired.

Everything looked good, but I saw no sign of any air marshal or other official who might be armed and in a position to defend the flight. Most law enforcement types can spot each other in a hurry, and I saw nobody who resembled a law enforcement officer. Soon, one of the pilots came out of the cockpit and walked to the back of the plane. He tried to look casual, but he was doing the very same thing I had done: scanning the passengers. After he returned to the front of the plane, the second officer followed suit.

Having done as much as I could to spot a dangerous person, I went to the back of the plane to get a magazine. Two stewardesses were in the galley speaking softly. I leaned in and whispered that I was a 26-year veteran of the FBI. They requested my row and seat number, and it was obvious they were quite pleased about my presence on the plane. Even though it had been years since I'd carried a gun and a badge, I was confident that I knew a lot more about security and self-defense than most of the passengers and crew.

After we landed safely, the crew came to me and thanked me profusely. I had really done nothing more than let them know I was on the plane. But if things had turned bad, I could have drawn upon my years of experience and training to assist the crew. Obviously, there is only so much one can do when faced with odds that multiple terrorists would probably have some weapons, whereas the crew and I were thoroughly frisked and disarmed at the magnetometer.

As I drove home, I began to wonder why the federal government was not tapping into the enormous pool of former law enforcement and military personnel who are part of every community. There must be thousands of us in every major city, and I know that the smaller towns have numerous former military because that's where a great number of our fighting men are recruited.

And so far, our terrorists have lived in larger cities—New York, for example—where it is impossible for people like me to own and carry weapons. Think of it: thousands of former law enforcement and military personnel, trained in security, most willing to do whatever it takes to protect our women and children, and our facilities, yet, federal and state governments have disarmed us.

Moreover, in the case of at least one federal agency—the FBI—they are turning down the good faith offers of former FBI agents to do volunteer work—any unpaid work—including answering the phones or even taking out the trash just so that a contribution of time can be made to fighting the terror that faces us all.

Why are these obviously good resources being ignored? Simple. As a society and government we are still thinking inside the box of pre September 11, before we were so terribly attacked on our own soil. The ramifications of that attack have not fully sunk in. Everyone should be on the lookout, but trained law enforcement officers, now retired or in another profession, are able to do more.

Many eyes watching and ears listening is a good thing in times of war. Thousands of former law enforcement officers armed and engaged would be a terrific infusion to the already over-taxed law enforcement agencies straining under the weight of enormous terrorism investigations, trying to back-fill the vacancies in the ranks caused by military call-up.


# It Can Get Silly

Airline passengers are now subjected to intrusive searches and long delays at airports, but they don't mind when these searches and delays make sense. I've seen grandmothers and grandfathers searched, old ladies mortified that foreign-looking security guys without a high school degree are rummaging through their carry-on bags.

Teenage kids, clearly of Anglo, African or Latin descent are touched with hands and electric wands by guards determined to find the nail-clippers. Smokers lose lighters at the magnetometer so that they can't light their shoes, and everyone nods approval because nobody wants to die. One senior congressman had to drop his trousers recently to prove he had a hip replacement! Good folks cooperate, grimly inching forward in long lines, hoping the U.S. government knows what it's doing.

But more and more are recognizing that the U.S. government is not really doing the job well—yet. Some fear it's going to take more deaths, along with the death of the airline industry as we know it, before our leaders get it. And if the airline industry goes down, our economy will be damaged for a long time. Our hoped-for recovery will simply disappear.

As I waited to board my plane, I was reminded how confused, selfish, and gutless bureaucrats and politicians are. I noticed a Middle Eastern man, between the ages of 20 and 35, in the waiting area. He had a carry-on bag between his feet. He was not behaving in a manner that would make me suspicious, but his appearance was enough. He was a match.

He fit the profile of the terrorists who had hijacked the aircraft in September. I reviewed what I knew. He had arrived at the airport and was stopped by the police officer at a first checkpoint where he produced evidence of a flight, plus identification. Those two items anybody can get easily. The officer had to notice he was a match. I'll assume he checked the man as thoroughly as he was allowed.

Next, the man had to go through the magnetometer, and obviously he got past that review. Again, I assumed the screeners noticed he was a clear match.

But the real breakdown of security began when he entered into a large waiting area where vendors, maintenance workers, other passengers, and bag handlers mingled. He could go into the men's room and be alone in a stall where he could retrieve an object left there for him, or he could meet a co-conspirator. I think it's fair to assume that the cleaning crew has not been given a thorough background investigation. Would the airport security search through every tub of cleanser? What about the many vendors who were doing business in the room? Many had the look and clothing typical of Middle Easterners. Do they hate America? Are they related to any of the terrorists?

There was one last precious chance to catch this match before he boarded his plane. But the gate-screener and the airline employees followed the orders they have been given by the FAA: they selected benign-looking passengers—at random—for a complete bag and body search, while the Middle Eastern man, who fit the terrorist profile, ambled down the walkway to the plane.

When I boarded, he was sitting in the very first seat of the coach section, a prime place from which to launch an assault against the crew or cockpit.

They left him alone, because to single him out would have subjected them to criticism. They were not ordered to search every Middle Eastern man of a certain age. Why? Because the federal government has avoided this issue due to the continuing insanity of political correctness.

Political correctness has trumped safety, security, the national economy, our common sense, life itself—everything.

It's up to our leaders to put a stop to this insanity before more people die. I'll wager that another airline terrorist attack will destroy the airline industry, and our fragile economy along with it.

And if the media and Congress would talk about this threat as much as they talked about Enron, I'm certain we'd finally get the FAA on a war footing. We're still playing games with American lives, determined not to offend anybody. This is madness, and it must stop.

## And Then, Ridiculous…

Could a G.I. Joe doll turn out to be dangerous?

Recently, my nine year old nephew and his mother traveled from Richmond, Virginia, to Newark, New Jersey—by plane—to visit the city and pay their respects to Ground Zero, the hole in the ground where the Twin Towers existed before September 11, 2001.

My sister-in-law, Beth, is as Irish in appearance as one could possibly be. Her freckles and her facial structure shout out her ethnic heritage. Likewise, her towheaded boy could never be mistaken for a youthful suicide bomber. Nevertheless, they were in for an unpleasant experience while catching their flight home.

She made the mistake of going by F.A.O. Schwarz, the famous toy store, to treat her son David to a small toy as they were leaving for the airport. Full of patriotism after visiting the site of the horrible terrorist attack, David selected a G.I. Joe World War II Medic Kit. Inside the small, colorful box was a miniature canteen, a first-aid box, some dog tags and a one-inch pistol made out of black plastic.

As they made their way through security, mother and son were inexplicably separated by two security guards. Beth was taken off to the side and the search was begun. She was very concerned about being separated from her son as it was a busy and confusing process. She turned to look back at him.

The security guard, busy going over every square inch of her body with that dreaded wand, ordered her to "face straight ahead!" Maybe some would think my sister-in-law overly protective, but she disobeyed the order and looked back at her son, who was at this point also being frisked aggressively.

Her guard shouted, "I told you to look at me! Do not look at him! Look right at my face!" With that, the guard who was looking through young David's belongings, shouted, "Gun!" as he held up the offending G.I. Joe Medic Kit.

She slowly, gingerly extracted the tiny plastic weapon from the box, as if it could possibly go off, and held it aloft for all to see! What a discovery! Good job! The two guards immediately shut down their security line, totally humiliating my sister-in-law and bringing tears to my terrified nephew. He later told his mother that he thought he was going to throw up. He was sure that he had done something terrible.

Airline travel is more than getting from place A to place B, and it used to be fun. It's not fun anymore. People who travel for personal reasons use airlines strictly as a necessity, but I predict that this optional way to travel will soon go the way of the buffalo, caused by government over-reaction, ordered by mindless, stupid bureaucracy. Who needs it? Moms and dads will simply stay home, take a train, or drive to their vacation spots.

The newspapers and airways are filled weekly with similar stories of Gestapo-like conduct at our nation's airports. A former presidential candidate—an old man now—was totally humiliated when he suggested that they "do have time to get him on his plane." The airline in question had invoked the inflexible 30 or 45 minute show-up rule. Some airlines allow less time to board aircraft, some allow more time. Who can possibly keep up with this?

Another older gentleman—a World War II Vet—became annoyed after being subjected to yet another full body search. When the guard was rifling through his wallet pulling out every card, every piece of paper the exasperated traveler asked, "What do you expect to find in there, a rifle?" He used the dreaded gun word! He was promptly arrested and charged a hefty fine. Needless to say, he and his embarrassed wife missed their flight and had to take another one the next day.

Not long ago, my wife and I were flying back from Long Beach, California, to Dulles, Virginia. We watched in astonishment as the first person searched was a 93-year old black grandmother in a wheelchair! Her daughter tried to help her but was shooed away by the guards. They forced this poor old woman to stand up and remove her shoes. We watched in horror as she wobbled in her effort to comply. Would she fall? Would she break her hip? Not this time, thankfully.

Did we feel safer? No, we felt totally helpless and disgusted. Given a chance to make our airports and airlines safer, the political party that's supposed to know how to make things safer, has blown it. There is an absence of leadership in the way these searches and security measures have been created and implemented. Everybody knows it, and lots of folks are saying it. Why won't the White House pay any attention? I say fire Mineta. I don't care what ethnic minority he belongs to; he's acting like a moron!

If airport and airline security is symbolic of how this nation moves aggressively to protect its citizens, it's a resounding flop. Anybody who travels by plane today can look at the system and see its obvious flaws. For one thing, the entire concept of searching passengers before they board an aircraft is built entirely around the concept of political correctness. Heaven forbid we make any Middle Eastern young men uncomfortable or hurt their feelings! It's so much easier to search the Irish woman, the young kid, the World War II Vet, or the 93-year old wheelchair-bound grandmother.

I think the federal government is killing the airline business with this nonsense. But there is much more at stake for the political party who is in charge of our new, improved airline security system. If politicians can't think of the obvious reason to fix this mess—to catch real terrorists—perhaps they can think ahead to election time when a very annoyed traveling public will use their vote to indicate what they think about the federal government's best attempt to make airline travel safer.

The government's job is to make airline travel as safe as humanly possible. But, it's every citizen's job to let their political leaders know when things are not being done in a common sense fashion. Silly searches at an airport protect nobody, and the airline industry suffers. Smart searches that don't adhere to Hard-Left politically correct notions of what constitutes profiling, will protect us better.

# *The Lessons of Patrick Henry*

The stories of these border skirmishes, which yet live in the traditions of the West, are highly worthy of collection. They exhibit scenes of boldness, craft and ferocity, on the part of the savages, and of heroic and desperate defense by the semi-barbarous men, women and children who were the objects of these attacks...of the almost incredible achievement of women and little boys...of the capture, captivity and torture of some...

William Wirt's biography of Patrick Henry was begun in the summer of 1805, six years after Henry's death. Wirt's book captured the lives of Henry and many of the men and women around him in a precise and wonderful way. Wirt presents a snapshot of what life was like before, during, and after the American Revolution.

This old book may contain lessons for us, if only we will allow history to be our guide.

We learn that colonial life was always hard, made harder still with a force of British soldiers becoming increasingly impatient and belligerent with American colonists. For their part, these colonists were weary and irritable from scraping out a living while fending off hunger, violent Indians, the beasts of the forests, unseen and incurable diseases, and finally, the British tax man who was determined to mine these hard-working independents for all they were worth.

At a point in time, our relatives would tolerate no further abuse, and they acted to take control of their own lives and destinies. Patrick Henry led both rag-tag colonists and elitist leaders like Washington and Jefferson to a decision which has produced the greatest nation on the face of this earth.

Most school children today, however, are unaware that the purpose of Henry's *Liberty or Death* speech—for which he is most famous—was to convince the timid, cautious and undecided that it was time for Virginians to arm themselves and form up into groups of citizen soldiers who would repel the ever-increasingly violent British.

A country was formed around the pillars of liberty and faith, where honesty and non-violence became the norm, as colonists collectively agreed to respect the law. For those citizens who would not restrain their lawlessness, there were the officials in the cities who would investigate, arrest, and punish them.

But just in case, the citizen-soldiers held on to their guns. They vowed they would never be treated as helpless victims again, and to make sure, they wrote gun ownership into the Constitution. Patrick Henry led that march as well. He would not allow Virginia to ratify the Constitution until a promise was made to include a Bill of Rights. And those rights are almost exactly the same ones that were adopted by Henry's beloved State of Virginia years before.

It was safe in the cities, but quite a different scene out in the countryside where colonists, ever pushing westward, were plagued with acts of violence by the Indians who believed that the Great Father had reserved the lands for them. Of course, there were always the bears and other beasts to look out for, and hunting put meat on the tables.

Wirt's book documents a destructive dynamic that concerned Virginia Governor Patrick Henry: the colonists who were attacked by the Indians were caught up in an endless tit-for-tat war that seemed to have no end. Just as the hostilities would seem to die down, groups of colonists out on a hunt for meat for the table, would not pass up a chance to stop by the nearest Indian settlement and attack, just on principle.

The Indians would soon visit the colony to return the favor. When the men were off hunting or engaged in some other activity, the Indians would attack the log cabins. But, quite often they were repelled by the women and boys who were well armed and fully trained in the use of firearms.

Unlike the more peaceful cities where the constables on patrol could rush to the scene of a disturbance, it was impossible for the government to protect women and children in remote log cabins and little villages. These innocents had to defend themselves, and they did!

Time has passed, and now historians with a bias against American traditions have served up a sterile history to our students, where men are the aggressors, owners of slaves, and abusers of Native Americans. Women have been all but airbrushed out of our history by the revisionists, because to talk of them would reveal their courage, their protection of family homestead, and their brave hearts, which in large part have made this nation great.

What a difference a couple of hundred years make. Most would agree that the crime today is not in the countryside, but is to be found where the cops are most plentiful still, as Americans blithely abandon so-called inner cities for the safer countryside.

But, if crime has changed its base of operation, our society has not yet caught up to the changes. As we read and watch in horror the endless parade of the raped, the mugged, the stabbed and the murdered, bleeding down the pages of our newspapers, staining the minds of our young children, we wring our hands just as the colonists did pre-Patrick Henry.

And the victims then are the very same victims today, except these days it's politically incorrect to suggest that a woman do anything dramatic to protect herself. We give them phone access and some memorized numbers, then lie to them by saying they're safe.

Back then, when it was actually safer to be alive, society gave them guns and taught them how to shoot. It is my guess that years ago a man would think twice before he attacked a woman. Today's violent predator can count on the average woman being unarmed. Some call this progress. I call it society's failure to protect those who need protection the most.

Terrorists' attacks launched against targets on these shores killed victims without regard to gender. Many women are taking this opportunity to arm themselves. Have we finally realized that self-defense is just as important a right as the ones Patrick Henry endorsed?

## *Let's Remember Patrick Henry*

> They moved vigorously, their rifle barrels and tomahawk blades glinting in the morning sun, their voices charging the air with liberty songs and patriotic exhortations in the neighborhoods they passed. —H. Mayer
> *A Son of Thunder: Patrick Henry and the American Republic*

Patrick Henry, one of America's greatest Founding Fathers, has been nearly lost in our nation's history. I wonder how many school children are taught about his political courage. Perhaps it was Henry's plain talk that has irritated historians to the degree that our schools teach so little about him. After all, he symbolized free speech, and in that symbolism can be found the seeds of discontent with bureaucratic authority—a threat that surely strikes fear into the hearts of educrats, everywhere.

Educrats want children to find fault with most traditional things. Parents, religion, and American history are all fair game for a reexamination and a critique. But teachers who question the ethics of George Washington for owning slaves, or Christopher Columbus for bringing disease to these shores to infect innocent natives, will never encourage a close examination of their teaching methods or performance by students, or anybody else.

No wonder they would not want to encourage students to think and speak like Patrick Henry. Henry questioned authority. The government schools don't want that!

During his famous St. John's Church speech, Henry cried out, "Give me liberty or give me death," and therein, begged Washington, Jefferson, Randolph and other giants of the day to give him authority to form a well-regulated militia. Henry knew there was a need to fend off the British through force of arms. They had become increasingly hostile to the freedoms and commercial interests of the colonists. Henry knew that without weapons and men there would be no hope for a revolution, and Henry wanted a revolution like no other.

Revolution meant freedom and liberty, and liberty was the "crown jewel." Without the basic freedoms, men would be slaves to the state, and without the right to bear arms, men would always be looking over their shoulders against the day that an oppressive central government could take freedoms—take everything—away.

After his stirring speech—perhaps the most inspiring speech in American history—Henry was granted the authority and was made chairman of the militia plan. But unlike most of today's leaders, Henry went on to implement his plan in a most dangerous and dramatic way.

Days after the shot heard around the world in 1775 in Concord, Massachusetts, Virginia's British governor, Lord Dunmore, ordered British troops to seize the arms and gunpowder kept in the battery in Williamsburg, Virginia. Word of the seizure soon circulated among the Virginia colonists and was mixed with the news of uprisings in Concord and Lexington.

This news proved to be explosive, yet it was mere outrage without the lit fuse of courageous leadership. Even though many had assembled and insisted upon strong action, the leadership held meetings instead.

Naturally, the moderates wished to take the wait-and-see position, thereby avoiding further aggravation of the governor. They were afraid.

Hearing of Dunmore's seizure of the colonists' arms, weapons that protected the colonists' families against all manner of danger, Henry rushed to one of the assemblies, and in his typical take-charge manner, spoke publicly the reasons the governor's actions should not go unanswered.

So persuasive was Henry that the men insisted he be made commander of the militia on the spot. They bestowed upon him the trappings of the typical patriot of his time: a tan hunting shirt, a rifle and musket ball, and a single Indian tomahawk for close-in fighting.

Together, with Patrick Henry now in the lead, hundreds marched smartly on Williamsburg and right into our history books. Governor Dunmore, perhaps a better reader of tea leaves than a warrior for British interests, immediately caved in to Henry's demands and made restitution for the stolen arms.

Patrick Henry was a passionate man who held the ideals and realities of the young country always in mind. He realized then that the right to bear arms would allow the colonists to break free from the clutches of a controlling British monarch.

Years later he would break from Washington and Jefferson when he insisted that our new Constitution include certain rights, including free speech and the right to bear arms. Henry knew that without fundamental freedoms, the nation had little chance of fending off a strong central government's greedy advances.

Patrick Henry gambled everything on a single idea and because of his incredible vision and courage, a nation basks in freedom, liberty, and prosperity today. Of course, Henry's path to freedom was paved with arms and ammunition.

We can't be teaching our kiddies about those nasty, awful guns in school, now can we?

But it is the right to bear arms that keeps an ever-growing bureaucracy mindful of the awful cost if it ever tried to enslave its own citizens. That's why the Hard-Left works so hard to disarm us. They know they will never reach their final goals without a disarmed, compliant citizenry. That's precisely why Patrick Henry and others insisted that the Second Amendment be adopted—to fend off despots like those who surely exist within the Hard-Left today.

# CHAPTER NINE—
# Clinton/Gore Post Script

In a recent C-SPAN survey, the nation's top historians ranked President Clinton as the worst scoundrel among all U.S. presidents, hitting moral rock bottom below Richard Nixon and pro-slavery leader James Buchanan.

Overall, Clinton ranked an average 21st, just ahead of Jimmy Carter (22nd), a one-term president who is widely regarded by scholars as a good man soiled by an unquestionably failed presidency.

Bill Clinton rated 20th in Crisis Leadership; 21st in International Relations; 21st in Administrative Skills; 22nd in Vision/Agenda Setting; and 21st in Performance in the Context of the Times. His lowest scores were in Relations with Congress (36th) and Moral Authority (41st), the lowest possible score.

Historians were not alone in their low assessment. Two other surveys asked the opinion of the public. C-SPAN viewers likewise ranked Clinton at the bottom for moral authority, but otherwise rated him even more harshly than historians. Viewers rated Clinton as 36th worst overall, with rankings below average for every category except economic management (19th) and public persuasion (15th). By the way: Ronald Reagan, the president the Clintons love to hate, was ranked in the top 12 of all presidents!

The verdict is in, and for a president so concerned with his legacy, the news is not good. Clinton may have escaped removal from the White House in 1998, but he will never escape history. Clinton has tarnished the White House in ways previously unimaginable, and time is only likely to further reveal the true extent of the damage done.

To make sure we as citizens get all the truth about the Clinton legacy, we need to support institutions, authorities and organizations that clearly demonstrate through their words and deeds, a desire to know the truth. A growing number of Americans at last understand that the truth—often quite disturbing and ugly—is something to seek, not a crazy uncle to be hidden away in a closet.

# *Moving On*

It's ironic and a bit unfair that Vast Right Wingers like me are still hounded by individuals who insist that we drop the entire Bill and Hillary issue because it's time to move on. A walk past any newsstand with a pensive Bill Clinton plastered on the cover of *Newsweek* or *Time* seems evidence enough that it is not we who refuse to move on.

Inside, we will find another puff-ball article that permits Clinton to put the best spin on every lousy thing he did. Clinton tries to blame his amazingly bad decisions on politics, still unwilling to admit that he did anything wrong. He *will* admit that he made bad political decisions, but even *that* he excuses as victimization—he was given bad advice.

In these endless opportunities Clinton is given to explain, we will learn that the bad-rap Clinton is now receiving is caused by the "permanent Right Wing establishment" who "felt entitled to rule." Evidently, according to Clinton, "we live in an historical period when the fanaticism of America is on the Right, and it has an apparatus to support it." He claims that the Vast Right Wing has been determined "to deny his legitimacy as president from day one and sully every part of his record, even after he left office."

Now, why is it that he feels his record has been sullied? Is there reason for he and his victim wife, Hillary, to feel sorry for themselves? Have they truly been wrongfully accused by this now "permanent" (no longer "Vast") Right Wing, victim to vicious attacks?

Let's take a minute to recall the record of our former president, given so much attention since he has left office.

The first time I ever spoke to Bill Clinton, he was trying to put a smiley face on Waco. The Branch Davidian complex had burned to the ground and 20 or more children had died a horrible death. Nevertheless, he told me that Waco was a mass suicide. I looked into his eyes and saw...nothing—no sympathy, no remorse, no care, no feelings at all for the children. I only saw a disconnected coldness.

I had seen that look before in the eyes of sociopath criminals who laughed as they stole the life savings of little old ladies. I put a number of these con-man types away. They were all the same—they would not admit that they had done anything wrong, even in the face of overwhelming evidence.

Of course, we found out later that it was Clinton's White House that pushed Attorney General Reno to get the Waco standoff ended in a hurry. Why? Because Waco was causing Bill Clinton political embarrassment, and he wanted it over. So, a fumbled, hurried plan ended up killing the guilty, but not without many innocent lives lost.

But can we condemn him for that? That was OK with Bill Clinton because it was all about politics.

I also recall Billy Dale, Director of the White House Travel Office, being framed by the Clintons. In an effort to avoid firing him (for fear of media retaliation), they attempted to use the Justice Department and the FBI to send an innocent man to prison. Why? Because Dale got in the way of Hillary's political plan to staff the office with her own people.

But Clinton didn't care that he was railroading an innocent man. He was doing it for political reasons, and that made it OK.

Osama bin Laden struck us in Somalia and then continued to kill our citizens all around the world. Clinton's response to these attacks were measured and timid actions that only encouraged bin Laden. But, you see, it was all about politics. Bill Clinton didn't do anything wrong. He simply took bad advice...so it must be somebody else's fault.

Perhaps we should overlook these wrongs, recognizing them as just politics, but when politics is exonerated above our national security, I cannot, *will not,* forget.

When I was able to get some answers as to why a president of the United States would be so blasé about national security, I became more concerned. It was in this area, I believe, that Clinton became most dangerous. My fear for the nation's safety and my anger were so great that it caused me to go public about the Clinton administration.

He and his followers—cultists, actually, when you consider that they would follow him anywhere and forgive him for just about anything—were willing to trade our national security in an effort to seek a bigger, broader political agenda that had less to do with the United States and more to do with the agenda of the United Nations.

My background is not in foreign relations, but I could see how much the Clinton administration was giving away to hostile nations. For example, they gave away our best technology and the most advanced computer equipment and access to our most closely guarded facilities. Meanwhile, they were busy downgrading, and in some cases abandoning altogether, the safeguards that prior presidents had built to protect American lives.

And *still*, they wonder what generates the keen interest of people like me who insist that somebody keep an eye on this amazing human being, Bill Clinton.

How can we let the Clinton matter drop when his friends in the media just cannot let him go? Why should we stand by silently and let the mainstream media airbrush Clinton's dismal record? Where is the virtue in remaining silent while his media friends try to rehabilitate this seriously flawed man's legacy?

As long as Clinton is praised for his legacy, we will continue to remind the public of the truth of this man's past. The fact that so many need to ask why we bother and why we can't move on, should do nothing but heighten our concern. As long as the mainstream media gives Clinton unlimited access to the general public, I shall not move on. Patrick Henry had this to say about history:

*"I have but one lamp by which my feet are guided, and that is the lamp of experience; I have no way of judging of the future but by the past."*

What was good enough for Patrick Henry is good enough for me.

# Senator Dim Bulb

And Hillary's legacy? It appears to be equal to her husband's! When I first heard the stories coming out of New York about Hillary Clinton's appearance at a fund-raiser to benefit September 11, 2001, victims, I promised myself I was not going to comment. At times like these one should resist making statements that tend to divide, I suppose. Yet, the thought crossed my mind that people are finally getting wise to her.

New Yorkers voted Hillary into office, so it's not my business to question their collective judgment. Still, one has to wonder if many a New Yorker isn't just a wee bit wistful about how it might have been if only Rudy Giuliani had been able to weather his health problems so that he could represent New York as an honest-to-goodness U.S. senator.

Still many others would say that you must stand where God puts you, and Rudy certainly did. Who will ever forget his leadership following that horrible attack? Who could voice a critical or unkind remark about his job performance? Even George Pataki, who few knew outside of the Empire State, rose to national affection with his reasoned, gentle manner, reminding us that some rise to leadership for good reasons.

And then there is Hillary. Just prior to her performance, where she received many catcalls and boos, she was known as the urgently important person whose motorcade ran down a police officer at her direction. The uniformed police officer was simply trying to enforce some security restrictions designed to protect us all.

Would that be just one of the reasons why New Yorkers and a whole lot of firemen and policemen were angry with her?

Or could it be that Hillary, not so long ago, pronounced NYPD officers, accused of violating a suspect's civil rights, guilty before trial? Her approach to members of law enforcement, I guess, is to hang them and then give them a fair trial. Most citizens of this country know that you are innocent until proven guilty—even the police.

Are New Yorkers angry because Hillary was probably behind the release of Puerto Rican terrorists? Or, maybe it was that very public kiss and hug offered to the wife of an international terrorist that tipped them off? And, didn't the Clinton White House play host to Gerry Adams, a well-known and very dangerous IRA terrorist? Maybe New Yorkers think Hillary is not the best person to appear at an event staged to support victims of terrorism?

Hillary's blind spot is not just politics. Here's a woman getting paid more than eight million dollars to recall in a book what happened during her eight years in the White House. The real curiosity about that book deal is that for nearly a decade Hillary testified under oath that she could not recollect anything important at all. Now we are to believe that she will write an interesting, fact-filled tome about those very same years. How did she get her memory back?

It's amazing she could not recall firing more than two dozen long-time White House employees, little old ladies in the Correspondence Office. I suppose they were in the way of Hillary's ambition to staff the White House with unqualified, undignified political hacks. With Hillary's guiding hand, the White House turned into a circus sideshow, plagued with moral and ethical problems instead of keeping the standard as the premier federal working office.

When she was finished with those brilliant moves, she ordered the firing of the White House Travel Office staff. In order to cover her agenda—to get those slots for her freak parade (to be fair, who else would work for this woman?)—she had her staff accuse them of federal crimes and was quite willing to see innocent civil servants off to the federal pen for getting in her way.

Then, her long-time friend, and some say intimate confidant, died of a gunshot wound (self-inflicted?), whereupon Hillary's staff vacuumed his office clean of incriminating and embarrassing documents that were found later in the Clinton's personal residence. But Hillary again claimed, even under oath, she had no idea how they got there.

Recall also that Hillary carefully selected our new attorney general, insisting that the post be given to a woman. She proceeded to embarrass all of womankind by first choosing one who knowingly violated federal immigration laws, coupled with another who skirted close to the same Nannygate problems but fell short of confirmation when certain U.S. senators asked if they could review her alleged Playboy photo spread.

Finally, Hillary settled with Janet Reno, who will be best remembered as a below-average prosecutor from Dade County, Florida, who was a fierce opponent of religious sects and willing to burn down villages to save the children.

Hillary's DOJ friend and soul mate Reno was also the nemesis of patriotic Cuban-Americans who dared to offer safe harbor to terrified refugee boys. Reno's feds rushed their peaceful Little Havana neighborhood with rifles on full automatic, as well as a rifle-butt-"hello" for any news media brave enough to photograph Reno's Gestapo-like tactics.

People who work for and around powerful people have the ability to recognize the real thing from a phony. I don't know a law enforcement officer who respects Hillary Clinton. They resent her serial lies under oath and understand how corrosive the corrupted-powerful can be to law and order. Is that why they hissed and booed Hillary?

No, their distaste goes far beyond that, and I'm not really sure one can actually put a finger on why Hillary is so disliked. Call it a cop's instinct, if you like. Actually, who cares why so many people despise Hillary Clinton? They just do.

## First Shot across the Bow

Many people have asked me when my war with the Clintons first began. I remember that day so clearly. I had written an article for the *Wall Street Journal* about the many FBI files Craig Livingstone had managed to grab before his activities were discovered. When the article first appeared, my residence was swamped with reporters from just about every major newspaper. Here is my first professional writing assignment, in its entirety:

"I loved my career with the FBI and treasure my years as a special agent. Of the many assignments I was privileged to have over the course of my 26-year career, the highlight was the five years I spent assigned to the White House just prior to my 1995 retirement.

For more than three decades the FBI, the Secret Service and the White House Counsel's Office had worked as a team to clear the hundreds of new staff members who came with each new administration. This clearance process entailed a lengthy FBI background investigation to document the good character of every White House employee. It was a comprehensive and effective security system, perfected by six presidents to protect national security, the taxpayer and the White House itself.

But the things I saw in the last 2½ years of my tenure deeply distressed me. And the recent disclosures that the Clinton White House requested, and the FBI provided, more than 340 background investigations on previous administrations' employees, raise questions that pierce the very heart of national security and call into question the relationship between the White House and the FBI.

Some presidents have made good use of the FBI background investigations, and some, to their regret, have not. But never before has any administration used the background investigations of another president's political staff. FBI employees knew it would be wrong to give raw FBI files on political opponents to the other party. In fact, they knew it would be illegal; each disclosure is a violation of the federal Privacy Act.

Why, then, did the Clinton administration request such files, and why did the FBI provide them? The White House's explanation—that it was "an honest bureaucratic snafu"—is really too much for this FBI veteran to believe. How does a unit at FBI headquarters copy and box for shipment to the White House Counsel's Office more than 340 highly confidential files, when the two FBI superiors are both lawyers? Do the White House and the FBI really expect us to believe that the wholesale copying of hundreds of FBI files wouldn't raise an eyebrow? That the two FBI supervisors didn't know who James Baker was? If the FBI supervisors didn't know that hundreds of confidential files were going out the door, they were so grossly negligent as to imperil not only the civil rights of more than 340 individuals, but also national security.

In truth, I know that FBI management has plenty of warning that elements of security and background investigations were drastically wrong at the Clinton White House. As early as May 1993, Special Agent James Bourke, supervisor of the FBI office responsible for background investigations, had come under fire when, at the behest of the White House, he started a criminal investigation of seven innocent men in the Travel Office.

Not publicly known until now, were the constant warnings that Mr. Bourke and other FBI management received from me and my partner, Dennis Sculimbrene (who would go on to testify against his own agency and the White House as a defense witness in the Billy Dale trial). Why are Mr. Bourke and the good folks at the FBI now finding serious reasons to check on the legitimacy of the requests of this White House? Documents exist that prove they have known about these problems for years. Mr. Bourke declined to be interviewed for this article, so one can only speculate as to why he ignored repeated warnings. It may be that, like any bureaucrat, Mr. Bourke was simply trying to win favor from those he thought could advance his career, in this case, White House officials.

These allegations are more serious than anything we have seen in decades. So how can the White House, through Attorney General Janet Reno, be allowed to order the FBI to investigate itself? No federal bureaucracy is good at conducting an internal probe that has this kind of potential for explosive revelation.

Right up to the time I retired in June 1995, Mr. Bourke and other FBI supervisors responsible for background investigations continued to honor each and every outrageous request made by the Clinton White House Counsel's Office. Mr. Bourke cannot claim he did not know these requests were improper. He was well aware that the Clinton administration had relaxed the security system at the White House so that those loyal to the administration could evade background checks. Other agents and I had told him so, and scores of documents going across his desk provided more evidence, just in case he did not believe his own agents. In fact, at the time the White House requested the files on previous administration's appointees—one full year into the Clinton administration—more than 100 Clinton staffers, including Press Secretary Dee Dee Myers, still had not been investigated by the FBI for passes or clearances.

Yet the Clinton White House Counsel's Office apparently was wasting no time looking deeply into the background of anyone who was not lucky enough to have been hired by President Clinton. As Mr. Bourke also knew, permanent White House employees whose loyalty to the Clintons was in question were in for some special attention—Hillary Clinton style. For example, permanent employees in the White House residence who were suspected of being disloyal to the first lady were reinvestigated out of sequence—that is, early—in some cases, four years before their periodic review was due.

Some of these staff members, appointed by Presidents Carter, Reagan or Bush, had just been cleared by the FBI. When I attempted to head off what appeared to be unnecessary and premature investigations by offering to obtain copies of the background investigations, my superiors at the FBI and Craig Livingstone, director of security for the White House Counsel's Office, effectively told me to mind my own business. What prompted the White House to investigate these staffers was a story, leaked to the press, that Mrs. Clinton had thrown a lamp at the president during a domestic argument. The Clintons had to discover the "leaker."

The result was that decent, loyal, law-abiding citizens with spotless records were investigated by the FBI again, just to make sure. I believe that these permanent employees were being harassed, and that if anything, anything at all, had turned up in a new FBI probe, they would have been summarily tossed out the door to make slots for the Clintons' people. And indeed, other employees besides Billy Dale were fired on the basis of these investigations.

At the same time, the White House was requesting copies of FBI investigations of hundreds of long-gone Reagan and Bush staffers. Why? Knowing the Clintons casually used the FBI to weed out politically suspect employees, would it be so unreasonable to suspect them of also misusing the FBI to investigate political enemies? Statements by Clinton spokesmen that nobody looked at these FBI files are as plausible as saying that if 340 Playboy magazines were sent to a boys' high school, they would remain in their boxes, unmolested.

The safe where these secret records were allegedly kept was the size of a small bedroom. Maybe the files were taken out of the safe, maybe they weren't. There was no need to take them out to examine them. Anyone—including Mr. Livingstone, whose desk was just outside the entrance to the safe—could have walked in, sat down at the table and perused the files to his heart's content. And, the security office was equipped with a photocopy machine. I knew Mr. Livingstone was a fierce defender of the Clintons, especially Mrs. Clinton, who handpicked him for this sensitive position.

Which of these files were copied, and where were the copies sent? The time has come for real explanations, real investigations of the Clinton White House Counsel's Office and, sadly, maybe even of the FBI. In particular, Mr. Bourke and Mr. Livingstone should explain their roles. These FBI files could not have been requested, received and maintained without Mr. Livingstone's full knowledge, consent and direction. Mr. Bourke is responsible for protecting the FBI files and for ensuring the FBI's arm's-length relationship with this or any administration.

These two men should be brought before both a federal grand jury and Congress to account for this highly irregular conduct—conduct that has embarrassed the presidency and the FBI, undermined the public's trust in both institutions and potentially violated federal law. The Clinton administration has earned its reputation. But the FBI—my FBI—deserves better. Enough is enough."

## *Agents are Obliged to Take a Bullet, but Not the Fifth, for the President*

After my article in the *Wall Street Journal,* I was attacked nonstop by the Hard-Left, and many others, some well-meaning, who had discomfort with the idea of an FBI agent working inside the White House deciding to tell the truth about a corrupted president. The matter of disclosure by a federal agent finally came before the Supreme Court and the answer was made clear for all to read, if not to accept.

The question put before the court was, should those who are charged with protecting the security of the president and the executive branch tell the truth about dangers to that security, and could they be compelled to testify before an independent counsel's grand jury?

The answer to both questions was "yes," particularly when alleged high crimes pertaining to the president and his closest advisers were involved, and the chain of command does not respond to repeated warnings from line agents on the scene.

As in the Nixon era, the issues before the court of public opinion center on serious allegations of criminal conduct at the highest levels of the executive branch, including obstruction of justice, subornation of perjury and conspiracy to commit both.

But another presidential administration better exemplifies the dangers to national security when Secret Service agents remained silent—even as they determined that the president's behavior placed him and national security at risk. Seymour M. Hersh's recently released book, *The Dark Side of Camelot*, about the cheap and reckless conduct of President John F. Kennedy, has added a new wrinkle to the discussion.

For those who question my motives for writing my own book, Hersh's study should illustrate the exact reason I spoke out—not only was the security chain of command silent about the grievous security breaches they knew existed in the Kennedy (and Clinton) administration, but so were the national media. In the case of the Clintons, this dangerous phenomenon dates back to the 1992 campaign.

The *New York Times* weighed in with a lead editorial concluding that federal agents working at the White House are obligated to go public and to appeal to the media whenever they are aware of serious wrongdoing but are unable to get their superiors to respond to real concerns for national security and the safety of the president.

Ironically, the *Times* wrote this startling opinion seven days before former intern Monica Lewinsky had her last visit with President Clinton in the Oval Office, a visit he denied under oath. Of course, in 1996 the *Times* had no use for me and my revelations.

During the Kennedy administration Secret Service agents saw the national security threat the president's behavior created. The agents duly reported their concerns up the chain of command, and political concerns prevented any real action—a mirror image of the circumstances I faced as an FBI agent serving in the Clinton White House. I received no backup support from my own agency, even though there were documented cases reported to FBI headquarters that should have been setting off alarm bells.

In both instances where the Secret Service ignored national security scandals and the FBI management stiff-armed senior agents assigned to the White House, rank-and-file agents believed that bringing the dangers into the light of public scrutiny would have finished their careers. Does that make it acceptable to permit important national security information to die on some bureaucratic vine? Of course not. But, if agents know beforehand that their information simply will be ignored, whom are they truly serving? Have they fulfilled their oaths as sworn federal agents to defend the Constitution?

Obviously not.

An important question comes to mind from an historical perspective. If the myth of JFK had been debunked in the beginning, and if the media had not been so willing to compromise their mandate to report the truth, would the nation have suffered so much from his death and the decade of violence and protest that followed?

The four Secret Service agents who went on the record for Hersh made it clear: when agents charged with the security of the president and his office are prevented by the behavior of the president from performing their jobs, thereby placing the chief executive and national security at risk, there must be an official avenue available for them to alert not only their superiors but also the congressional overseers and the American people. Does this proposal of openness jeopardize the security of future presidential administrations? Absolutely not. For too long, citizens have labored under the misconception that the president is accountable to himself alone and that executive privilege means executive immunity from law enforcement.

Interestingly, in Hersh's book, Secret Service agents attached to Kennedy spoke at length about their frustration not only with his behavior, but with the laissez-faire attitude of his closest advisers toward long-held national security procedures. Kennedy saw his Secret Service detail as fellow golf-club-swinging, drinking-buddy womanizers out for a good time—at the expense of the taxpayers (and the first lady). But the agents observed those same serious lapses in protocol when the administration dealt with matters of diplomacy.

When agents objected, Kennedy booted them out of the White House or they simply left in disgust. How was the Clinton administration any different?

Why has it taken 30 years for the Secret Service to talk about Kennedy's dangerous behavior? Why did a Secret Service director find it necessary to publicly scold four retired agents when they did speak out? Secret Service directors and other agency managers had good reasons to question the retired agents. If rank-and-file agents ever started talking about the Clinton administration, the stampede of Secret Service bureaucrats out the door would have created a serious draft.

In fact, the real reason Secret Service management wanted line agents to keep their mouths shut was to protect management's collective backside.

And, FBI management was no different when I was in the Clinton White House. The national media's painful failure to report the news as it happened and their almost maniacal hostility when I published my book has identified a great gulf between the nation's leaders and the American people. In fact, while Clinton's approval ratings remained high, public opinion turned downright angry toward the national media. There is an important lesson to be learned here, and I hope that the national media will hear it.

Placing themselves in harm's way had a new meaning for Secret Service agents in the Clinton era. When agents were called to testify before the congressional oversight committees investigating Filegate, they were faced with a real dilemma. Congressional investigators asked pointed, tough questions about the mysterious appearance of 1,200 confidential FBI files in the White House. Under oath, administration officials had blamed the agents for the mistake. Called to testify, the agents were candid and forthright. It was impossible, they maintained, for the files to appear in the White House due to an error on their part.

The Clinton administration paid them back for their honesty. Within weeks, the Justice Department announced its intention to pursue criminal and civil charges against the agents for a host of alleged wrongdoings, including perjury and evidence-tampering. The charges were dropped, but not before the agents were thoroughly discredited and dismissed or had resigned under a cloud. Such was the price for betraying the president, and the administration wanted to make sure everyone was on notice: lie, remain silent or be professionally destroyed.

Are these options the proper alternatives for those line agents charged with protecting any president and national security? In situations such as this, a clear distinction can, and must be, drawn between the two interests, particularly when presidential safety means covering up for illegal activity. (Of course in times of war, different rules come into play.)

Those charged with protection of national security and the safety of the White House occupant are charged with taking a bullet for the president, not taking the Fifth Amendment for him.

And, Bill Clinton didn't figure into his calculations the Supreme Court, or one FBI agent who believed what he read in the Constitution.

# Ken Starr and Robert Ray

I'm asked about the reasons Bill and Hillary Clinton were never made to answer for their notorious conduct, especially when they occupied the White House. Many people believe that they broke laws, or that laws were broken by their subordinates at their direction. Ken Starr and his successor, Robert Ray, apparently failed to find anything to prosecute. Ray eventually got around to issuing a report on Filegate, perhaps the most blatant abuse of power during the Clinton administration.

Nobody I know was pleased with the findings of Starr/Ray, and I believe most honest Americans could not be pleased, given its contents and conclusions.

Nearly four years after the discovery that violations of privacy of more than 1200 Americans in the FBI file-stealing case occurred, Mr. Ray wrongly concluded that the entire matter was caused by "the gross incompetence of the mid-level White House staff and the laxity of eager-to-please FBI officials."

Amazingly, he bought Hillary Clinton's story that she did not hire or even recommend the hiring of Craig Livingstone! Gross incompetence in this matter was not defined by the actions of FBI or White House officials—but by Starr's and Ray's office! For example, it took more than 30 workdays for Starr's office to begin an investigation of the theft of FBI files. By the time FBI agents finally went to the White House to interview witnesses and do a crime scene search, whatever evidence might have been laying around had surely been made to disappear by the culprits involved.

Moreover, credible organizations, including The Patrick Henry Center, objective media, citizen activists and our sometimes effective Congress, uncovered massive evidence of wrongdoing and wholesale lying by the Clinton White House that took place on a continual basis. This mountain of evidence makes Starr and Ray's findings beyond ridiculous.

Furthermore, how Mr. Ray could find any former or current Clinton White House employee or resident more credible than your average FBI or Secret Service agent has to be the eighth wonder of the world! Mr. Ray missed or ignored important evidence, some of it very new—all of it very credible. But believing Clinton White House officials—all of whom were lying, Hard-Left politicians—over sworn federal agents with no axe to grind is remarkable.

For example, I was the first to report to the public that Hillary hired Craig Livingstone, in my book, *Unlimited Access* (page 36), long before it was an issue. My partner, Dennis Sculimbrene wrote an official FBI report about Hillary's connection way back in 1993, long before the true nature of the corruption at the White House was suspected.

Other federal agents made statements under oath to Congress that the FBI files were obtained illegally, for no good reason, and told of their knowledge of the hiring of Livingstone at Hillary's command.

Which one of these credible witnesses appeared in Ray's grand jury? Not one! Starr and Ray's failure to obtain our sworn testimony allowed Ray to smear us—to punish us—by claiming Ms. Hillary, and a former bar bouncer, and a disgraced White House counsel, were credible, and by implication, we were not.

Of course, Ms. Hillary, Mr. Nussbaum and Mr. Livingstone denied everything. So, there you are! Believe them—notorious in their ability to lie or spin the truth—or believe sworn, experienced, mature federal investigators. You choose.

Mr. Ray made his choice—a horribly wrong one—but the question is, why? Did he suspect James Carville was about to do to him what he did to Ken Starr? What else could possibly explain Mr. Ray's mistake? Did Mr. Ray make any of his decisions based on simple human fear?

He could not have made his decisions based on the evidence. For example, we now know that a large number of Clinton White House e-mails referencing the Filegate scandal were hidden from investigators. According to one person who saw the e-mails, "if their incriminating contents became known, people in the Clinton White House could go to jail."

The Starr/Ray investigation and its wimpy report was nothing but an expensive, disappointing, wasteful failure! It calls into question the federal government's ability to police itself. With un-policed corruption on a scale so obvious, who protects the general population from abuse from its own government? It's an important question.

# *Attempted Theft of an Election*

The dirt that we had dealt with for eight years was certainly not all that was in store for us, even after Clinton left office. After the close of the presidential election in 2000, all the tools of the Hard-Left were brought out again. Gore's conduct was reprehensible, but if he had been able to steal the election, the general population would have eventually gotten over it.

The mainstream media would have made sure of that. Nevertheless, after the terrorist attacks on our country on September 11, 2001, most citizens were relieved that Gore had lost, including a great number of Democrats who had been hysterical in their complaints that Bush had stolen the election.

But it was a well-kept secret that Al Gore and his vice presidential staff were no better than Clinton's in looking out for America's interests, if quality of staff was any measure. Gore's staff—at least the ones I saw through my investigative lenses—were cut from the same cloth as the previous administration, and in some cases, they were remarkably worse.

Therein was one of the major differences between an Al Gore administration and a George W. Bush administration. Staff is policy, as every White House historian knows.

Many of those above the rank-and-file of our national security agencies were helpless to prevent the Clinton/Gore security collapse. Maybe they were too afraid or unable to believe the reality of a purposeful monkey-wrenching of the system. So, unopposed, the Clinton/Gore administration did exactly what it wanted to do, and as a predictable by-product, the outrageous and debilitating scandals took place—and the laptops and nuclear secrets walked off to who knows where.

Those in the system, the security professionals who claim today that they have no idea about how these security breaches took place, are simply lying. As an effective lightening rod, Bill Clinton and his staff took much of the heat, but Al Gore and his senior staff had major security problems of their own, mostly ignored.

Worse, Gore and company were fully aware of the White House-wide security collapse, and did nothing to prevent it, even when they were warned that it was happening. As a former senator, Gore should have been more concerned about it, but there is no evidence of concern. Gore did nothing but defend Bill Clinton, regardless of the impact on the nation. Thank God he was not elected.

It was Al Gore's Reinvention of Government initiative that first publicly complained about the security system that had been an effective screening tool for more than 30 years. Gore and his people deemed it too complicated, too expensive, and too intrusive to the applicants wanting to work for the federal government. So, they ordered agencies to privatize much of this important work, turning to outside contractors in many cases.

As a result, career national security professionals like me left in droves, having had our responsibilities taken away, our jobs downgraded, or our positions eliminated altogether.

We saw the benefits of Gore's "improvements." For example, almost one million background investigations backed up at the Department of Defense as a direct result of Gore's Reinvention schemes. Gore constantly used the term "risky" to define the plans of others, but my former associates tell me that identical problems existed in every important national security agency or system.

In other words, Gore and company took an effective security protection system and helped break it. But if Reinvention came with serious risk, Gore, the ever Hard-Lefty, will never admit it.

Mainstream media focused on administration-generated sound bites about personnel reductions and budget cuts. The truth is, when Bill Clinton robbed the national security bank, Al Gore drove the getaway car.

This is what I wrote during the 2000 campaign about the Clinton/ Gore presidency:

> The security personnel they've cut and the money they've saved to make themselves look better will form the basis of a gigantic bill that will be presented to the next president—unless, of course, that president is named Al Gore. In the event that Gore takes over where Bill Clinton has left off, you can be sure that he will do nothing to reveal his role in the greatest national security calamity since the bombing of Pearl Harbor.

After September 11, it's quite appropriate to acknowledge the obvious: there is no Republican administration in modern times—if ever—that failed to make national security a centerpiece of their time in office.

For me, a security professional who worked in both a Republican and Democratic White House, there can be no hesitation. When it comes to national security, the Hard-Left that I've worked with just doesn't seem to get it. Why?

In my opinion, it doesn't matter much why they tossed out national security. If you can't prove they crashed the system for treasonous reasons, then what matters now is that we can, and must do to protect what we have left.

During the campaign I also stated that "along with real protection of national security at the White House, the obvious by-product will be a relatively scandal-free White House."

But before George W. Bush could become president, the Hard-Left put the entire nation through an expensive and traumatic exercise designed to steal an election, or at least undermine the new president's ability to lead.

# War... Without the Guns

After the presidential election in 2000, I wrote the following piece as the nation struggled to make sense of what the Hard-Left was doing.

"They have no shame. They excuse oral sex in the Oval Office, and they excuse federal violations committed by any one of their leaders. They think that everything is fair, as long as they can win. They believe that politics is war, without the guns.

They don't care if you dislike them or disrespect them. They are not seeking your approval.

In fact, they hate you. You stand for traditional values. You crave and promote honesty. You are old fashioned, out-of-step, boring, and a fuddy duddy. You're naïve; you're intolerant. You hate gays and blacks and Hispanics, and the homeless, and poor people, and you mean to destroy the environment. That's what the Hard-Left believes about you.

And they are going to stop you from having power by using any technique, any trick in the book.

They are in full battle mode right now.

Somewhere in Florida and Tennessee they've set up war rooms to conduct a full scale attack on this election, and they mean to take victory away from George Bush no matter what they have to do.

You must stop hoping, wishing, or even praying. That will not help now. There are no last minute horse soldiers coming over the ridge to rush to your rescue. God is not coming here to defend us against this attack. Besides, God helps those who help themselves! Pray if you wish, but then act!

You must understand that they will lie. They will bribe. They will accuse the Bush campaign of doing exactly what they themselves are doing, and they will not blush or be embarrassed to make allegations they know are absolutely false.

Even now they are laying a foundation for this bloodless coup. They have already told you that Al Gore will not concede. Al Gore has already told you that he will not concede. What more evidence do you need?

For their part, the GOP is already running for cover. With all the foundation laying going on right now by the Gore people to steal this election, instead of Republican leaders going on the offensive, they are hiding under their beds, wringing their sweaty hands, having conference calls, or focus groups, or conducting polls. They are doing everything except taking the offensive!

They are letting us down again!

After the sordid Lewinsky affair was discovered the Democrats had eight months of absolute silence from the GOP during which time they successfully framed their argument that 'it was only about sex.' Thus the Impeachment was doomed to failure from the beginning because of the GOP's unbelievable wimp factor.

The Democrats will do it to us again, unless each and every one of us acts now. Not tomorrow, not next week, not after we wait to see what happens. We must act now!

Aren't our leaders tired of bending over and grabbing their ankles? Frankly, I'm embarrassed to watch them do it over and over again. Will they ever stand up to be counted? Do they know what political courage is?

They must act now!

Illegal votes? What about the millions of illegal aliens who have been made into proper little democrats by the crooked Clinton INS? The Democrats laugh when they recount that so many of their voters live in a graveyard. They think it's funny! Voter fraud? They invented it, and they are the only ones doing it!

Why can't the GOP say something? Say anything! Lead, for goodness sake! Do what you're getting big bucks to do! Fight for us, for our country! This is not just about politics, and if you don't understand that, please step aside and make room for those who do.

Friends, please, I beg you, communicate with your leaders, your congressmen, your senators, and your contacts and friends within the GOP and tell them this:

If they stand silently by and let Al Gore and the crooked Hard-Left steal this election, then we will do what we have to do: We will storm the gates of the GOP at every level, and we will overhaul this ineffective, bureaucratic, lackluster organization in ways that will shock even the most hardened democratic warriors. Tell them that even James Carville and George Stephanopoulos will be impressed at the political bloodbath that will take place if the GOP lets us down again.

We've had enough! Let the cry be heard all over this nation that the GOP must get its act together now! Everyone is thinking the same thing, but is too polite to say it, so I'll say it —this election should have been a slam-dunk!

Now we're supposed to stand politely by and have this hard-earned victory snatched from us by schoolyard bullies who have never grown up?

I don't think so, and here's my message to the GOP: Lead, follow, or get out of the way!"

# *Suddenly, the People Assembled and Spoke!*

Congress shall make no law respecting an establishment of religion, or prohibiting the free exercise thereof; or abridging the freedom of speech, or of the press, or the right of the people peaceably to assemble, and to petition the Government for a redress of grievances.

More than three decades ago, the Hard-Left marched, and yelled, and shouted, and threatened. They also demeaned, and cursed, and they threw human feces at the "pigs," and called for their deaths.

They burned American flags while saluting the Red Chinese, the North Koreans, Fidel Castro and North Vietnamese officials. Today, very few Sunday news show's talking-heads say much about it, other than to remark that these outrages were evidence of democracy in action.

Many media talking-heads (some obviously fond of their radical pasts) amazingly agree that the Hard-Left's often violent and highly objectionable, illegal activities were the natural, appropriate, and pre-dictable conduct of "peaceful war protesters." There isn't any conduct, it seems, that deserves condemnation by the mainstream media, as long as that conduct is used in the furtherance of Progressive Liberalism.

But behold! Let a few well-dressed, well-mannered angry Conser-vatives "assemble peaceably" to protest the theft of a national election, and the scolds on the Left (and sadly, a few on the Right) line up to question their motives and decry their tactics after being led gullibly in that direction by a former peaceful war protester.

I understand the Hard-Left's knee-jerk reaction.

Those of us who have long memories will never forget the Sixties, a time when the raised middle digit was a well-known way for thou-sands of Lefties to honor our flag, our president, our institutions, the CIA, the FBI, and the thousands of men in uniform who were dying in Vietnam.

But it was their constitutional right to do most of those things, even if their rude and violent behavior caused many of us to want to throw up.

In one Sixties march on Washington, D.C., the National Guard set up 50-caliber machine guns in the hallways of the Department of Justice, fearing that more than 500,000 peaceful war protesters would overcome the guards at the gates. These Hard-Left rioters, now re-called as peaceful war protesters, were intent on burning the hated place down.

Meanwhile, a young Bill Clinton was leading an anti-U.S. parade on foreign soil, a "general" engaged in a very well-organized and orches-trated peaceful war protest.

Wholesale destruction of cities, universities, banks, indeed any place which symbolized tradition or American values, was the order of the day, as the Hard-Left used, then misused, the First Amendment to push their socialistic agenda forward. Where was the mainstream media then, and do they remember any of this now?

Those illegal riots, rallies, or violent marches—those less than peaceful gatherings of the Hard-Left—worked! Over the years the Hard-Left has scolded, whined, threatened, shouted, bullied, bludgeoned, harassed, intimidated, coerced, bombed and burned their way into power.

Who could ever forget the armies of Black Panthers, as they waltzed around with high-powered rifles in an extremely violent display of anger and hatred?

Astonishingly, yesterday's Second Amendment warriors are today's gun-hating pacifists, but in those days, weren't you in fear of your lives and your property? You bet you were! How afraid were you of the 2000 election protesters in Miami with their Dockers and department store Polos with those cute little horses?

Did short hair, ties and good manners cause you to hide your children from the TV set? Did you recoil at their well-articulated shouts, slogans free of Sixties-style obscenities, and the absence of threats to your well being? Were you shocked?

Or, were you gladdened like I was, to see some Baby Boomers, and others who represent your point of view, marching on our streets for a change!

Make no mistake about it! The Hard-Left meant to shock and scare you when they conducted their rallies. Theirs' was a well-known, often-used political tactic. In fact, they perfected the use of shock, anger, and hatred, and they are using those same tactics still.

And it upset them when we used some of their tactics—even if we were polite and kind, but especially when we were winning!

The Hard-Left shifted the politics of this nation dramatically toward the left in ways that many believe illegitimate, but where were the media scolds then, to point out that this was not the American way? Where are they lately? Have they conveniently forgotten the crudeness, the rudeness, the violence or the hatred?

The Hard-Left in the media may have forgotten, but many of us never will. Why? Because we must not! Because the Democratic Party has embraced the dirty politics of the Hard-Left, and they have continually used these same tactics to attack and defeat those on the Right.

And, they used those tactics in an attempt to steal an election in broad daylight!

Senator Joseph Lieberman was on the lawn of our Vice President's mansion mourning the lack of civility in Dade County, Florida. On soil protected with the spilling of much American blood on foreign battlefields, Lieberman used ground on which he had no legitimate claim.

Lieberman, now referred to as "Sore Loserman" by our friends at Free Republic, brazenly stated that there was something illegitimate in the way that a few concerned Dade County citizens took loud and vocal exception to laws that were being broken by Dade County officials!

You see, the good citizens of Dade County decided to object to the blatant, illegal attempt to take a vote examination into closed rooms, thus forbidding access to news media and the general public. For some reason, Lieberman thought that their objections were a serious problem.

Nobody was arrested, nobody was harmed, and no property was taken or broken. This was the very essence of peaceable assembly and free speech, and yet Lieberman went on to demand, "Vice President Gore and I call on the demonstrators, and all who may be organizing or encouraging them, to stop these activities immediately. And I hope that Governor Bush and Secretary Cheney will join us in this call."

An appropriate reply to Lieberman's obnoxious statement might be, "Stuff it!"

Years ago, the citizens of Dade County insisted that "government in the sunshine" was what they wanted, so they passed numerous laws to guarantee that important government business was always conducted in the open—in the sunshine.

This way corrupt government action could be kept to a minimum, and partisan mischief could be minimized. When an attempt was made to hide the process from the people in this case, the people strongly and vocally objected. Rightfully so, Joe!

Speaking of years ago, what was Joe Lieberman doing with his spare time in the Sixties? On August 8, 2000, Tom Baxter, a reporter writing for the Cox News Service, gave us some hints:

> In his younger days, Lieberman organized anti-war rallies, but the mature man is identified among the Washington

scolds who decry violent video games, dirty rap lyrics and other signs of moral decline. That's part of the reason he's a good antidote to Clinton.

So, the same Senator Lieberman who seemed hurt, repelled, shocked and afraid of harsh words spoken in Dade County, once worked with the likes of Bill Clinton to organize mobs, to encourage violent rioters—rioters who then spit on cops, ripped and burned draft cards, turned over police cars, and in many ways gave the rest of America the finger!? Say it isn't so, Joe!

All this time we've been led to believe that a future Senator Lieberman was working on his Orthodoxy, while pondering the ways violence might be curbed. What a fraud!

If there's anything true about today's Democrats, it's this: Hard-Left Democrats are notorious liars, obnoxiously brazen thieves, and hypocrites of the highest order.

Sadly, this group now even includes "Holy Joe, the conscience of the Senate."

It's sad and pathetic how thoroughly power corrupts! But America can be grateful that Gore and Lieberman were not in charge on September 11, 2001, and if polls are any indication, most are.

Of course, being on Clinton/Gore Watch was not always dismal business. Sometimes there was some real humor to be enjoyed. For example, when I heard that former President Clinton might agree to get a real job.

## *Clinton Radio Talk Show Only Urban Myth*

The rumor that Bill Clinton might become a radio talk-show host was pure urban mythology. This preposterous idea had to be nothing but myth because talk-show hosts have to work hard.

For a moment, let's entertain the idea that Clinton actually does become a radio talk-show host and is able to drum up a listening audience. I've come up with some important topics and events for him to cover on his first 10 shows:

- PETA's 1st Annual Pig Roast

- O.J.'s arrest of the real killer
- Haitian go-go economy
- American Trial Lawyers Fairness & Ethics Club
- Hollywood's 50th wedding anniversary dance
- Abortion Associations' Festival of Life
- Eco-Terrorists' Log-Cutting Contest
- Hillary's Marriage Counseling Clinics
- *Washington Post's* unbiased, factual news reporting
- Bill Clinton's War on Terrorism

Well, it might be dubbed a comedy show, but it will never happen anyway. Why? Because I believe Bill Clinton will never do real work a day in his life. He will never hold down a regular job. He will never show up on time, nor could he show up on a regular basis. Bill Clinton thinks having a job and a regular schedule is a lifestyle for chumps like you and me.

I saw the same attitude expressed by many of the criminals whom I interviewed and arrested over the years. In fact, several told me that it has been their life-long goal to fix things so that they would never have to work a single day their entire life. Many were able to pull it off without getting caught.

Of course, this meant that they constantly schemed to steal, con, lie, or do whatever else it took to get what they wanted. They adopted this approach to life early on and never strayed from it. Many of these cons were likable people and fun to have around, as long as you kept one hand on your wallet and an eye on your wife. The criminals I knew in my FBI career were very much like Bill Clinton, and these people exhibit nothing more than the behavior of a sociopath.

It makes perfect sense to sociopaths to live this way as long as they are not arrested or put into prison where they belong. Each and every day that they are allowed to walk the streets without having to do any real work is a reinforcement of their belief that the rest of us are simpleminded chumps and that they alone are the smart ones.

I never met a Mafioso who did not think he was brilliant. I never met a con-man who did not think the rest of us were the stupid ones.

Bill Clinton will never be a radio talk-show host, or have any other kind of regular employment. He's a con and a leech and will walk—no, will run—away the second it's clear there is real work to do.

# CHAPTER TEN—
# Closing Thoughts

## *Get Ready for Really Bad News*

If you think you've been bombarded by bad news, you haven't seen anything yet.

The Hard-Left is out of power, so there is only one thing they can do: lie until it hurts.

But Republican control of the White House, the House of Representatives and the U.S. Senate does not mean that those who suffer from Anxiety Disorder are giving up their hold on academia or the media.

These two extra-governmental, single-party powerhouses will certainly influence what happens in our politics in the coming months and years. Better get ready for a virtual tsunami of depressing news stories, statistics, scientific studies, and disasters predicted by Hard-Left-influenced or controlled computer-driven models.

Eventually, if you're not totally miserable and afraid, it will be due only to your understanding of what the Hard-Left is always up to.

The Hard-Left has no agenda; at least not one they'll admit. All of their socialistic goals have been achieved, and now much of the population is wise to it. That the Hard-Left wants to make us even more Socialistic will not sit well with the general population, and the Hard-Left knows it. That's why they have been losing in the election booth.

And that's why they loved and protected Bill and Hillary. The Clintons were such good liars! And they need liars to keep their movement alive.

If you are a Hard-Lefty, it's not a good thing for too many people to be well-informed with the truth, because Hard-Lefties make their living and derive their power from the arena of Leftist politics, which must include generous lies on a daily basis.

The Hard-Left feels threatened, and therefore, those citizens that have no clue what the Hard-Left does, or why they do it, will be running for the Prozac before the liberal hand-wringers are done with them.

If you're prepared, you'll not only weather the blizzard of bad news that's surely coming, but you'll be able to prosper from it. Future news stories to watch out for include:

Pockets of secret homeless people out there that somehow have been overlooked. Yes, it's true. The homeless population has grown no matter what we have tried to do, and now—and until we get another Democrat in the White House—millions of homeless will die! And if they don't die, they will freeze! Or, if they don't freeze, they will be starving and need medical attention!

Also, in a future news story we will learn that for some unknown reason, the homeless have brought millions and millions of innocent women and children to live with them on the grates of America's cities.

In fact, did you know we have more homeless children on our streets than Rio or Calcutta? You will learn this, and more, in a future news story.

The reason you didn't know any of this is because when Bill Clinton was president, the homeless were housed and well-fed. With a Hard-Lefty no longer in charge, the numbers of homeless has grown exponentially and now include gobs of children.

In another future news story you will be told that AIDS has somehow leapfrogged from a population of reckless gay men to the rest of the population, and of course your children are at immediate risk. Also, countless thousands of heterosexual males and females are now infected or are at risk of infection—they just don't know it, but the Hard-Left will tell them.

Of course, we'll be told that it's the fault of the Republicans because they are mean and nasty to gay people. It will be inferred that there is only one way to cure AIDS: elect Democrats.

That's because it's been determined through the use of sophisticated computer models that a *bad attitude* toward this very serious, pressing problem causes the AIDS virus to migrate to population groups heretofore unfairly protected against infection.

And watch out, we'll also be told that El Niño and La Niña have gotten married. Well, not really, but these two global weather phenomena have somehow gotten together to produce little Niños and Niñaettes!

These heartless, deadly weather offspring will produce floods on one coast, and drought on the other. We'll learn that we're in for global warming in a way that will fry your tamales for sure! That's not all—we also will suffer from global cooling, and there are experts lining up to tell you how this is possible, and *why this terrible thing is happening to us!*

It's because the insensitive, intolerant Republicans have cut off the funding for the various studies that always prove that Hard-Left Democrats care more about these things!

Better get your umbrellas ready, because skin cancer cannot be far behind, and don't try hiding inside your SUV.

Crabs in the Chesapeake Bay are dying, eel grass is wilting, endangered pup-fish are going belly up, and that nuclear power plant near your neighborhood is starting to vibrate!

Hard-Left Democrats can prove this and all other calamities known and yet to be discovered, with junk science, statistics, polling, and focus groups—which is the same as junk science.

And it's the Republicans' fault. Especially Bush!

Republicans may occupy the White House, the House of Representatives and the U.S. Senate, but they don't—by God—have Big Entertainment or Academia!

So now folks, war or no war, we're going to be punished with bad news, unless we can reveal the Hard-Left—this shady, angry bunch—for who they really are: sufferers of Anxiety Disorder.

The trouble with people who suffer from this newly discovered mental disease is that they cannot tell a phony threat from a real one. This makes them dangerous.

You may think I'm kidding, but we have a new psychological disorder being announced at least once a week. Why would it seem so inappropriate to label people who are liars, cheats and hysterics addicted to power and money, as those ill with some type of mental disorder?

If we call it Hard-Left Anxiety Disorder, can we discover a drug for it?

## *Thirst For Power*

Have you noticed how ruthless the Hard-Left has been in the pursuit of power? How willing they are to lie, distort, and deceive to get it? That's domination. Have you noticed their breathtaking hypocrisy? My personal favorite is Clinton cheerfully signing the Family Values Week proclamation in front of the cameras on the very day he and Monica first played with a cigar. That's a special kind of twisted manipulation.

You've probably noticed how uncompromising the Hard-Left is in wanting to spend more of your money. Spending your money provides them with the power to retain power. No way are they willing to give that up—it would mean decreasing their control.

I've always thought it useful to distinguish politicians by whether their true goal was to do well for themselves or for others. The selfish politician wants to do well for himself. Exhibit A is of course, the Clintons. Were they better off after eight years in office? They now have three mansions and a $200 million library/home, and that's just what we know about. These two have done well. Exhibit B is Jesse Jackson, shakedown artist extraordinaire, who reportedly has a slush fund estimated to be worth hundreds of millions.

This Hard-Left man also has done very well for himself.

The unselfish politicians, in contrast, are motivated by a desire to serve. They are not in business to get rich; they don't have to gain power by pitting one group against the other; they don't have to buy power by paying off pressure groups; and they don't have to lie, distort, manipulate or deceive to gain power; instead, they earn power by doing what's right. They tend to be Republican.

For the politicians whose goal is to serve, a part of their ethic is respect for the rule of law. They understand, even if only subconsciously, that without the rule of law, everyone is at the mercy of whoever happens to be the most ruthless in grabbing power. They also understand that if some public officials are above the law, then we don't have law.

This, by the way, explains in part why ethical people despise Clinton. It also explains why ruthless people who are only interested in their own advancement or self-indulgence, think Clinton is just fine.

After all, he's justifying their behavior, so it's the new norm.

But where does such behavior lead when you don't have the rule of law? We now come to an observation about what makes mass murderers tick. The answer is domination, manipulation, and control. If these are what motivate the truly selfish, and if, without the rule of law, the most ruthless of the truly selfish are going to be the ones who rise to the top, then where it can lead is murder on a scale that's almost impossible to imagine.

Hitler killed over six million of his people during World War II. Stalin killed 20 million of his people during the Terror. Mao was responsible for the deaths of at least 35 million of his people during the Great Leap Forward. History is full of killers who wanted domination, manipulation, and control, and they weren't constrained by law: Idi Amin, Tamerlane, Genghis Khan, Cortez, Pizarro, Pol Pot to name just a few.

The rule of law stands between us and atrocities on a scale that the mind cannot grasp. We don't have Hitlers or Stalins in this country, but undermining the rule of law is a slippery slope. Anyone and any group which undermines the rule is complicit in enabling the most ruthless and the most selfish to rise to power.

The more the rule of law is undermined, the worse, and the more dangerous, the leaders we will get. It's guaranteed.


## *If They Only Had a Brain*

Those afflicted with HLAD, or Hard-Left Anxiety Disorder, never tire of claiming that they're extremely intelligent. They always manage to elect "the most brilliant president in the history of the United States," and always claim to have "the smartest first lady the nation ever had."

Those with HLAD may be smart in some ways, but when it comes to protecting the homeland, they are exceedingly dumb. In fact, I have often said that having the Hard-Left in charge of our national security is a danger to us all.

Hard-Lefties have two major failings fueling their ignorance. First, they believe that anyone who is truly intelligent would be a member of the Hard-Left. Secondly, they have lousy memories. They fail to remember the lessons learned from history and are doomed to repeat past mistakes, thereby setting our nation up for disaster.

The Hard-Left adheres to a liberal pacifist ideology, even in matters of life and death. Our country is in a battle to the death with fanatical terrorists, and for a while, the Hard-Left was silent because they knew that if they openly criticized the president and his administration during a time of war, they would be toast.

That is, until a short time ago when a fairly impressive strike was launched against the presidency of George W. Bush, covered with the fingerprints of the Hard-Left. Key information was leaked and fingers pointed at the FBI. Soon after the FBI Phoenix memo was sent to other agencies, it turned up at the *New York Times* and the *Washington Post*.

The easy way out is to blame the FBI for the leak, except that it would be hard to find a single FBI agent who would trade George W. Bush for 10 Bill Clintons. So we must ask why the FBI would try to make Bush look bad? And consider this: why would the FBI leak a memorandum that would make their own agency look incompetent? But, facts don't matter to the Hard-Left; it's all about their political agenda.

Recently, the *Times* and the *Post* had headlines and identical information that was framed in such a way that citizens who didn't care enough to read deeper might conclude that George W. was not bright enough to "read the tea leaves" prior to September 11, 2001, and guess that our nation was about to be attacked.

The Hard-Left's attempt to bring President Bush's high poll numbers down didn't work, but they will keep sending up trial balloons to see if the citizens are bored enough to entertain another session of political street fighting here in D.C. If the lies continue, eventually, enough mud will stick. The Hard-Left uses the Big Lie all the time because it's one of the few arrows they have left in their quiver. They don't have any real ideas—all they have are accusations.

Now, there *are* those who will claim that the Hard-Left is not much different than the Hard-Right, but that's not true. One key difference between the two groups is that the Hard-Right had the evidence to back up their claims of a corrupt, and yes, *stupid* Clinton presidency.

Supreme Court decisions, federal grand juries, Independent Counsel reports, findings by federal judges and endless testimony in front of congressional committees and sub-committees, not to mention the accurate reporting of many news organizations, provided ample hard evidence of presidential corruption, recklessness and aimlessness.

Because the truth was surfaced, Bill Clinton is left to drag his legacy behind him with the ceremony and grace of an ogre dragging a hefty chain. Clinton's legacy was made without anybody having to fabricate a single fact.

Not only was Bill Clinton immoral and reckless, too often distracted by easy-to-get groupie bimbos, but during his administration the terrorists made steady progress toward September 11, surprising a new president with barely enough time in office to do a proper damage assessment of the agencies that protect us. In other words, Clinton was not asleep on the job, but he was *sleeping* on the job, with lots of women, young and old.

Bill Clinton didn't just squander his legacy—he squandered our *safety.*

Clinton made the Department of Defense, the Department of Justice, and other key agencies, dysfunctional. George W. Bush is still finding this out and fixing broken things as fast as he can. But what is one man supposed to do after years of purposeful neglect? Do citizens honestly believe that Bush, or anyone else, could fix in a short period of time all the things Clinton managed to damage or destroy in eight long years?

Of course not! And so, the American people support Bush in steady numbers as the repair work continues—and that's what worries the Hard-Left. They are desperate, and desperate people with poor memories and a propensity for lying, do desperate things, like endanger the safety of our nation simply to regain power.

They hate the fact that America's hero in the new millennium is a Republican. The contrast between the most corrupt president in history and one of the most popular and trusted presidents is obvious. It's no wonder the Hard-Left is determined to bring George W. Bush down.

Their bad memories prevent them from recalling that they orchestrated and cheered the cutting of defense and intelligence agency budgets and the doing away with human intelligence gathering techniques, all in the name of political correctness.

In fact, they have rammed political correctness down our throats to the degree that otherwise hard-muscled, steely-eyed FBI agents now sweat in all the wrong places at the thought of offending minorities by conducting investigations that could resemble racial profiling.

That's what the highly-intelligent Clinton administration did for the FBI—and that's just one agency. Political correctness killed thousands of Americans on September 11, and being PC continues to threaten our lives. But if you ask the Hard-Left, they will tell you it's Bush's fault.

If you could sum up the Clinton years you might conclude that the only thing Bill Clinton and his Hard-Left friends gave us was an inability to properly protect our nation.


# *Privacy at Risk*

What caused American society to pay particular attention to privacy issues in the 1960s and '70s? More importantly, what now causes the average person to yawn when Congressman Bob Barr and a precious few others try to warn us that our liberties and privacy are on the chopping block, being sacrificed to big business in the cause of commerce, or big government in the cause of national security?

FBI special agents have a keen awareness of the issues of a citizen's privacy. Federal law enforcement officers' training includes heavy emphasis on privacy rights, and after the academy, periodic training takes place on a field-office level to remind officers what data they can and can't gather about citizens during their investigations.

While I imagine the majority of well-trained federal agents are familiar with the Bill of Rights and follow the guidelines to the best of their abilities, believe me, they don't obsess on the topic of your privacy rights. The reason they are sensitive to this issue at all is because special emphasis on privacy matters occurred after Nixon held office and made for very lively conversations in law schools, prosecutors' offices, gatherings of defense attorneys, and anywhere a policeman or federal agent clocked in to get his pay.

Then, the Hard-Left was worried about your privacy. They had good reasons to complain about Big Brother back then but have maintained their silence recently as personal data is gathered daily as if we were being sucked clean of all our personal secrets by some enormous shop-vac.

The Nixon administration believed there was a Vast Left Wing Conspiracy determined to destroy America and bring him down. The FBI, along with so many other federal agencies, maintained files on thousands of campus radicals, many in business, and those in the media and Hollywood who had expressed anti-American views to the degree that they were believed to be subversive and quite possibly dangerous.

There were many minority groups who advocated and used violence to get what they wanted. Burning cities and exploding bombs were evidence that they could generate the kind of actions and riot-inciting rhetoric that any federal government would find a threat to national security.

The Black Panther Party, the Students for a Democratic Society, and many other radical groups were engaged in violent acts and acts of domestic terror too numerous to list here. Those who attempt to describe that era in our nation's history as the time of the peaceful war protester, or energizing civil-rights marches, are forgetting the violence and counting on the average citizen's disinterest in accurate history. Bad times are best forgotten.

The reason the federal government's feet were held so close to the fire after those years was because the FBI and other agencies were wiretapping the phones of the Hard-Left and conducting secret entries into their residences and places of business, looking for fugitives or evidence of conspiracies. What was true then is probably true today. It's likely that after eight years of Bill and Hillary Clinton, FBI files are full of notes and memos and reports about the activities of the Vast Right Wing Conspiracy. What the Clintons could not get from the FBI was quite possibly obtained through the use of former federal agents, now in business as private investigators, some willing to break a law or two for a high-paying client.

What are my grounds for such serious allegations? After the Oklahoma City bombing in 1995, the Clinton administration made much of a shadowy group plotting to commit more terrorist acts. After all, we had seen the lunacy of the Branch Davidians in 1993, right? They had a stash of automatic weapons hidden somewhere near Waco, Texas, and their leader was speaking gibberish, indicating a serious instability, so we were told. Four ATF federal agents died when search warrants were presented, and after violent resistance, the compound burned to the ground.

We had a mass murder-suicide in the name of religion on U.S. soil, and that's the way it was played. According to Clinton administration officials, the Branch Davidians were very dangerous. Two years later, Timothy McVeigh, and "persons unknown," blew up the Murrah Federal Building in Oklahoma City. This was a horrible and vicious crime, but hardly part of a pattern of activity.

As a result of this single act—and a lot of talk about angry white males—serious anti-terror legislation whooshed through Congress. Law enforcement and intelligence agency priorities were realigned, and suddenly there was a homegrown terrorist hiding behind every woodpile, or at least that's what the federal government and the media tried to tell us.

I wonder, whatever happened to all that intelligence gathered by the FBI and other agencies that were ordered by Janet Reno to investigate this "obvious and apparent" threat? Was that data loaded into the same computer that gathered all the data about a "nationwide conspiracy to commit violent acts" at abortion clinics?

If such information exists in some government computer, very few on the Right seem to care. Perhaps they have not figured out that someday an unscrupulous president, vowing to take revenge on her political enemies, may find use for such data. Did I say, "her"?

And as long as it was the Right that came under the investigative microscope, you can be sure that the Left and their friends in the media would be looking the other way on privacy violations. In fact, the entire discussion about privacy has suffered a slow and silent death.

That is, until now. With George W. Bush in the White House, environmentalists and animal-rights groups are being identified and investigated because they *really do* conduct nationwide conspiracies to commit property damage and violent acts! Burned buildings, busted out store windows, destroyed laboratories, and other highly destructive plots are just now being uncovered by the federal government.

And just as suddenly, the ACLU joins forces with Congressman Bob Barr in their concerns for our privacy. Bob Barr has been trying to protect our rights all along because Right, Left or Center, Barr understands the importance of the Constitution and the Bill of Rights and why these rights must be protected.

The Hard-Left has awakened from their Rip-Van-Winkle slumber and are now paying attention to potential privacy invasion and federal government over-reaching.

## Don't Ask for More!

I believe the time has come to insist that public officials put every law they propose through a common sense filter before they do any more damage to our present and future liberties.

Federal and state governments are rushing through legislation they say is designed to combat terrorism. Others say they are misusing their powers to hide the fact that they have failed us miserably.

New laws will not provide the safety we need and so richly deserve, but common sense will.

Frankly, I'm becoming concerned with the public statements made by some state officials concerning these new laws. One Maryland State Delegate recently said, "I realize that this bill basically says you can tap someone's phone for jaywalking, and normally I would say, 'No way,' but after what happened on September 11th, I say, 'Screw 'em.'"

No, Ms. Maryland Delegate, we won't let you do this! We won't let you take away any more of our freedoms—or get any more of our money—because you insist on being politically correct.

We have sent people like this arrogant, ignorant woman enormous sums of money and granted them amazing powers to protect us, and they have failed us. We have granted them state-of-the-art hardware and software to help them do their work, and they have let us down terribly.

They've told us—year after year—that they need many new employees and many new federal and state office buildings that cost more money. So, we sent them the money. They said they would hire the best people, but they told us they would decide who the best people are based on some politically correct social experiment. In the name of civility, and out of a sense of fairness, we let them do it, even though we knew it was a mistake to abandon the concept of excellence.

Over the years, and in spite of the failures, they've consistently ignored corporate models of success in favor of politically correct goals, and they've warned us—upon penalty of law—that a meritocracy was bad for America, and they would not permit achievement to be the deciding factor. We've allowed them to get away with a most dangerous fiction in the name of civil peace.

They've filled up ever-enlarging federal and state agencies with mediocre people who are rude to us and make huge mistakes—if they show up for work—and we turn our backs for fear that if we do not permit unacceptable conduct, some angry, revengeful mob will come to our cities and homes and…beat us up or burn us down.

They've blamed machines to cover their colossal mistakes saying there was a glitch.

They've told us that even though we sent them more money and bought and paid for the best new equipment and spent billions on special software, hiring more and more people, somehow they've ended up with useless, antiquated computer systems. How is this possible?

We possess in our simple homes the latest technology. Why is it that the federal government, with so much of our money, has hired so many employees working in so many big, palatial office buildings, but has had so many computer glitches caused by so many obsolete computers? Have they carelessly dropped their laptops on the marble floors of their spacious, opulently decorated offices? Perhaps they were momentarily blinded by a glare from the bubbling fountain just outside their satin-draped window?

They continue to lie to us—even today, after all that has happened—and tell us they had the brightest experts working on the problems. They've also had studies and hearings and commissions and meetings and talked and talked and talked.

Meanwhile, in 50 percent of our households, and in all of corporate America, Joe Six-pack and Suzi-Q blast along on the Internet, running circles around the government systems, and sometimes hacking into them just for fun.

My 14-year old daughter has a better computer system in her bedroom than the average FBI agent, and I'd venture say she knows more about how to use it.

But as the nice, naive, too-forgiving population that we have become, we allow this idiocy to continue. We've been too patient.

When we ask these self-important government officials why there are so many problems, so many mistakes, they say they don't know. We accept their non-answer, and we move on. We spend less and less of our money on our own children and compliantly send the government more of our hard-earned dollars. They've returned the favor by giving us less and less quality, and more and more trouble. Is there any doubt that it all came to a head on September 11, 2001?

People died because we have become accepting of mediocrity caused by political correctness—and this once mighty government of ours has become a parody of what the Founding Fathers intended. It's so big, so expensive, and so intrusive that it has now reached a point where many believe its out-of-control growth constitutes a significant danger to our way of life.

And yet our bureaucrats cry, "Give us more, give us more!"

The government no longer seems able to protect us; it has forgotten how, and its many conflicting laws, strung all over itself like some Lilliputianesque web, prevents it from doing what must be done. So, it does the only thing it knows how to do: takes away more of our liberties and more of our money. Meanwhile, we wait for New York City or Washington to become a smoking, radioactive ruin.

And yet as a great people, we hope for the day when we will cut the petty strings that bind us to inaction, woven by small-minded, self-indulgent tyrants, living off the public largesse.

They say it will take many more lost freedoms to get what we have already bought and paid for. Thank you for your blood, toil, sweat, and tears, but no, you may not have a refund. No money back, nobody fired, nobody even accused. It's government business as usual, post September 11.

We prove to these public servants over and over again that we love our country, our children and each other. We assure them that we would forgive their enormous mistakes—if only they would protect us like it says they should in the Constitution. Yet somehow, they do not possess the courage to do what must be done.

We insist that we especially love our Bill of Rights and want to keep the liberties afforded us there. We remind them that those guarantees make us the great people that we are. In return, these benefit-laden cynics glare and sneer at us, ignore us, and take away more freedoms. They even pass new laws to silence us. They accuse us of being anti-government when all we ever really were was pro-excellence.

And then, like the gentlewoman from Maryland, some of them even swear at us.

To her, and all the other arrogant bureaucrats everywhere who have become fat, lazy, stupid, and rude on *our* money and on all the powers *we* have granted them, and have the right to take away, let us say loud and clear, "Do not ask for more!"

No more of our money, no more of our liberties, and no more excuses for you!

Work with what we have already given you, and work as if your lives—and our lives—depend on it, because our lives really do depend on what you do.

But, if you insist on maintaining the politically correct direction that has been so destructive to this country, sooner or later many more of us will be killed—probably sooner.

## Summon the Big Thinkers

Fortunately, we have moved beyond the Clinton era, still picking up the pieces and reaping the consequences, but the good citizens of this country have seen to it that a Republican president holds office, and now, to the surprise of many, Republicans hold the majority in the House and the Senate.

There will be a period of time during which GOP leaders study the last election when the Republicans added seats to their majority in the House and took over the majority in the U.S. Senate. President Bush has finally established the Department of Homeland Security and is trying to move federal judge nominees through the confirmation process.

The Hard-Left had their day, and they made the most of it. Consider everything that has happened since the 1970s as just more frosting on the Hard-Left's cake—they achieved all their goals, and now their mission has become the maintenance of the status quo.

Even without a majority in Congress, the Hard-Left is not in bad shape when you consider they still control the powerful and influential Big Entertainment and Academia.

Is it enough for Republicans to smartly manage an unaccountable, ever growing bureaucracy? Is it sufficient to do that which the federal government is supposed to do anyway—to defend our shores from attack? What happens when victory is achieved? Do we then go back to our steady march toward Socialism, or is there more to being a conservative Republican than fighting and winning a war?

We know that this is a golden opportunity for change, but there seems to be no foundation for a "shining city on a hill," no clear vision for what we can achieve.

Republicans have rarely held on to power for very long. Recent history only confirms this. In 1994, the Republicans took the House and Senate, but Clinton had the White House and the veto power that comes with it. Newt Gingrich, a man of great vision, had achieved a great victory and became Speaker. Republicans got much of their Contract with America promises passed, but made significant compromises to get those through—and in the end, there was no son-of-Contract with America to inspire voters.

Republicans should remember this: for lack of vision, the power was lost.

The GOP achieved power again, only to have it slip away in a few short weeks when a turncoat liberal Republican senator switched sides and wrongfully gave the power back to Democrats.

This time it appears that Republicans will have the power for a while. We all know political change will eventually come and shift that power away, but isn't there some way we can hold on long enough to get the kinds of changes the majority of Americans want?

Existing inside the conservative movement are those who have a vision for a freer America, a more civil society, and a better-educated population. They know how to smart-size government. They know how, where, and when to cut taxes.

They can also solve most of our crime problems. They do not accept the lame excuses that have been used in the past by bleeding-heart Liberals to explain the reasons for decaying inner cities, teenage pregnancy, fatherless children, and destructive illegal drug use.

There are those who refuse to accept the relentless stream of sewage we call today's prime time television, where men openly urinate in front of cameras on network TV, and depictions of bizarre and incredibly violent bloodletting have become usual fare for millions of innocent children left to fend for themselves each evening.

Their parents return home late because both work just to pay the ever-increasing taxes, endless fees, permits, licenses, or union association dues. A lot of us understand that families are under heavy financial attack, and now we have a chance to come to their aid.

Let's not fail them.

There are great thinkers who have a vision of not only a kinder and gentler America, but also a stronger America that no longer takes constant grief or threats from tin-horn dictators in the name of accommodations. There are those who agree with President Bush that terrorists must be eliminated before they can migrate to our shores. Let's elevate these thinkers to positions of influence and power, and the sooner, the better.

Many believe it's time to take back some territory lost to Hard-Left Liberals. But positive change will never happen unless men and women who have a vision for a greater America are invited to the table and given positions of influence.

# Bibliography/Recommended Reading

Gary Aldrich, *Unlimited Access: An FBI Agent Inside the Clinton White House* (Regnery Publishing, 1998).

Saul D. Alinsky, *Rules for Radicals: A Pragmatic Primer for Realistic Radicals* (Vintage Books, 1971).

Mona Charen, *Useful Idiots: How Liberals Got it Wrong in the Cold War and Still Blame America First* (Regnery Publishing, 2003).

Danny O. Coulson & Elaine Shannon, *No Heroes: Inside the FBI's Secret Counter-Terror Force* (Pocket Books, 1999).

Ann Coulter, *Slander: Liberal Lies About the American Right* (Crown Publishers, 2002).

Kenneth deGraffenreid, *The Cox Report: The Unanimous and Bipartisan Report of the House Select Committee on U.S. National Security and Military Commercial Concerns with the People's Republic of China* (Regnery Publishing, 1999).

Joseph J. Ellis, *Founding Brothers: The Revolutionary Generation* (Vintage Books, 2000).

Darlene Fitzgerald-Catalan, *U.S. Customs: Badge of Dishonor* (Authors Choice Press, 2002).

David Frum, *How We Got Here: The 70's, The Decade That Brought You Modern Life—For Better of for Worse* (Basic Books, 2000).

Bill Gertz, *Breakdown: How America's Intelligence Failures Let to September 11* (Regnery Publishing, 2002).

Bernard Goldberg, *Bias: A CBS Insider Exposes How the Media Distort the News* (Regnery, 2002).

Daniel Goleman, *Emotional Intelligence* (Bantam Books, 1995).

Sean Hannity, *Let Freedom Ring: Winning the War of Liberty Over Liberalism* (Regan Books, 2002).

David Horowitz, *Radical Son: A Generational Odyssey* (The Free Press, 1997).

David Horowitz, *The Art of Political War and Other Radical Pursuits* (Spence Publishing, 2000).

Ronald Kessler, *The Bureau: The Secret History of the FBI* (Saint Martins Press, 2002).

Russell Kirk, *The Conservative Mind: From Burke to Eliot* (Regnery Publishing, 1953).

John Leo, *Incorrect Thoughts: Notes on our Wayward Culture* (Transaction Publishers, 2001).

G. Gordon Liddy, *When I was a Kid This was a Free Country* (Regnery Publishing, 2002)

Wayne LaPierre & James Jay Baker, *Shooting Straight: Telling the Truth about Guns in America* (Regnery Publishing, 2002).

John R. Lott, Jr., *More Guns, Less Crime: Understanding Crime and Gun Control Laws* (Univ. of Chicago Press, 1998).

Henry Mayer, *A Son of Thunder: Patrick Henry and the American Republic* (Univ. Press of Virginia, 1991).

William McGowan, *Coloring the News: How Crusading for Diversity has Corrupted American Journalism* (Encounter Books, 2001).

Barbara Olson, *The Final Days: The Last, Desperate Abuses of Power by the Clinton White House* (Regnery Publishing, 2001).

Barbara Olson, *Hell to Pay: The Unfolding Story of Hillary Rodham Clinton* (Regnery Publishing, 1999).

Bill O'Reilly, *The O'Reilly Factor: The Good, the Bad, and the Completely Ridiculous in American Life* (Broadway Books, 2000).

Michael Reagan, *The City on a Hill: Fulfilling Ronald Reagan's Vision for America* (Thomas Nelson Publishers, 1997).

Bill Sammon, *At Any Cost: How Al Gore Tried to Steal the Election* (Regnery Publishing, 2001).

Michael Savage, *The Savage Nation* (WND Books, 2002).

David P. Schippers, *Sellout: The Inside Story of President Clinton's Impeachment* (Regnery Publishing, 2000).

K. Alan Snyder, *Mission Impeachable* (Allegiance Press, 2001).

Some essays appeared on WorldNetDaily.com, Newsmax.com, and Townhall.com.

# The Patrick Henry Center
## for Individual Liberty
*Celebrating the life and legacy of a true patriot, Patrick Henry!*

## Our Mission

The Patrick Henry Center for Individual Liberty is a 501 (c) (3) nonprofit, charitable and educational foundation protecting and promoting the rights of all American citizens. In support of the ideals of Patrick Henry, the Center educates the public about his life and philosophy, and supports and promotes Freedom of Speech, as well as the other constitutional safeguards set forth in the Bill of Rights. The Center is dedicated to encouraging all citizens to "Stand Firm and Speak for America!"

## Our History

The Patrick Henry Center, incorporated in the state of Virginia, was founded in 1998 by former FBI Agent Gary Aldrich after he successfully disclosed serious corruption in the Clinton administration. His personal observations and experience compelled him to establish the Center to encourage and protect other ethical dissenters in their quest to surface the truth.

## Our Programs

*Whistleblowers:* Our flagship mission is assisting in the uncovering of serious wrongdoing in the federal government with special emphasis on national security.

*Patriettes:* An exciting new firearms program empowering women across the country to defend themselves!

*Broadcast!:* Voicing conservative values loud and clear and fighting political correctness in the media.

*House Managers Appreciation & Scholarship Fund:* Passing on the torch of courage and bold patriotism, as exemplified by the 13 House Managers, to the next generation of conservative college students!

Mr. Gary Aldrich frequently promotes The Patrick Henry Center's mission of educating the public on The Constitution, The Bill of Rights, and the rights of citizens' to engage in ethical dissent by appearing on numerous radio and television programs and speaking at a variety of events across the nation. For more information or for scheduling, contact us at:

### The Patrick Henry Center
P.O. Box 3449, Fairfax, VA  22038-3449
703.691.2301
www.PatrickHenryCenter.org

## The Patrick Henry Center Publishing Circle

The publishing of *Thunder on the Left* was made possible by the following generous donors.

### Friends of the Author

Mr. Roger Milliken
Mr. Robert Eichenberg
Mr. Paul M. Hammerbacher
Mr. Keith Twiggs
Mr. & Mrs. Bruce H. Hooper
Mr. John R. Cairns
Dr. Curtis Imel, DDS
Mr. Otto Kuczynski
Mr. Ralph G. Spencer
Ambassador Holland H. Coors
Mr. David N. Larson
Mr. Robert R. Fay, Jr.
Mrs. Janet R. Nash
Mr. Gerald R. Forsythe

### Patriot Publishers

Mr. & Mrs. Leslie J. Smith
Mr. James DeGanahl
Mr. James W. Gulick
Ms. Margaret B. Virkkunen
Mr. Terry A. Strine
Mr. James F. Fausek
Mr. Dante Stephensen
Mr. Robert W. Garthwait, Sr.
Mr. Robert Uhl
Mr. Joseph Gordon
Sentinel Utility Services of America

### Author's Ambassadors

| | |
|---|---|
| Mr. Christopher R. P. Rodgers | Mr. Dewey J. Levie |
| Mr. Robert L. Treanor | Mr. & Mrs. Tom Wenrick |
| Mrs. Donna P. Woolley | Ms. Mary Harding |
| Commodore Thomas J. Lupo | Mr. & Mrs. Ralph Scott Johnson |
| Mr. Jere Caldwell | Dr. C. Frederick Quest |
| Mrs. Alma M. Bowman | Mr. James Whitcomb, Jr. |
| Mrs. Mary Elizabeth Ewing | Mr. Elliot A. Baines |

Mr. & Mrs. Gerald Sirkin

Mr. William Eagleton

Mrs. Helen M. Smith

Mr. Arthur M. Downes, Jr.

Mr. Charles R. Sumner

Mrs. Mary C. Rohe

Mr. Victor H. Larson

Mrs. Terry Markham

Mrs. Barbara A. McBurney

Mrs. Patricia A. Still

Mr. N. T. Otterson

Mr. & Mrs. Robert Stringer

Mr. Ernest W. Beasley

Mr. Marvin P. Koenig

Mr. Lowell B. Yoder

Mr. A. F. Smith

Mr. Lowell B. Yoder

Mr. & Mrs. James T. Bourke

Mr. A. F. Smith

Mr. Kelly A. Grant

Mr. & Mrs. C. Frederick Miller

Mrs. Kathleen O. Harjes

Mr. John F. Milliken

Mr. Samuel M. Poist

Mrs. Mary Lou Almeida

Mrs. Geraldine K. Conover

Miss Marian L. Patterson

Mr. Robert L Moore

Mr. Lorance W. Lisle

Dr. David W. McDonald

Mr. Roger T. Hughes

Mr. Frank J. Vaughn

Mr. Leroy Weber

Mr. Saunders Jones

Mrs. Mary Jane Moffett

Dr. & Mrs. Peter H. Northup

Dr. Roy V. Maxson

Mr. Edward L. Whitney

Reverend James N. Cammisa

Dr. John W. Johnston

Mr. Andirs Kurins

Mr. Eldon K. Andres

Mrs. Mary I Hall

Mr. John D. Buhl

Mr. & Mrs. L. J. Whitmeyer, Jr.

Mr. Gene W. Hendrix

Mr. & Mrs. Carroll C. Misener

Dr. Hugo C. Pribor

Mr. Francis A. Madsen, Jr.

Mrs. George E. Atkinson, Jr.

Mrs. Jeanne C. Wulbern

Mr. Wilton J. Prejean

Mr. Carroll W. Anstaett

Mrs. Howard S. Perry

Mr. Leo M. Haverkamp

Mr. Myron A. Pennington

Mr. Donald T. Blake

Mr. Earl Lairson

Mr. Duane Hardesty

Mr. Kendall C. Miller

Mrs. Mitzi Perdue

Ms. Beverly F. Carter

Ms. Shelley Cohen

Mr. Herschell A. Cronkite

Mr. George L. Wrenn

Mr. M. Patrick Sweeney

Mr. Henry L. Wells

Mr. Einar L. Nelson

Mrs. Lee deLashmutt Thomas

Mrs. Doris A. Criswell

Mrs. Vera M. Hoskins

Mr. & Mrs. Henry F. Pellissier

Mr. Jack Rosenblatt

Mr. Kenneth H. Merry, Jr.

Mr. David L. Smart, Jr.

Mrs. Adeline R. Fudala

Mrs. Jean C. Walker

Mr. S. Wyatt Neel

Mr. Edward A. Lozick

Mr. & Mrs. Donald J. Walkwitz

*Mr. Walter E. Woelper*
*Mr. W. Robert Allen*
*Mr. James M. Newlin*
*Mr. James H. Lake*
*Ms. Francesca Scott*
*Mr. Kelly Hockema*
*Mrs. Linda Nail*
*Mr. Daniel B. Post*
*Col. Arthur B. Busbey, Jr.*

*Mrs. Kathryn M. Baker*
*Mr. & Mrs. Ernest T. Swinden*
*Mr. E.S. Ted Phillips*
*Mr. Michael L. Keiser*
*Lt. Col. R.E. Miller, USMC Ret.*
*Mr. Dennie Fugitt*
*Ms. Belina Lazzar*
*Mr. & Mrs. Joe Gallardo*

# Acknowledgements

Since this was not my first book, I knew the enormity of taking an idea and turning it into hundreds of pages of text, enough to satisfy thousands of readers hungry for the truth.

After my first book in 1996, many friends encouraged me to write another—I finally did—and so thanks must go out to them. But Leah Holcomb deserves special mention. When she came to The Patrick Henry Center as Communications Director, she had read *Unlimited Access*. She reminded me regularly that "it was time" to write again.

Once I had decided to write the book, the task of editing fell on Leah's shoulders. She did a magnificent job. Those who have never read, reread, and reread a lengthy complicated manuscript, have no concept of just how difficult that task can become.

A special thanks to Denice Jobe for reading over the manuscript to find those last minute changes that needed to be made.

The next challenge was to finance the publication. We had determined we should print and distribute the book and bypass the expensive services of a publisher, who usually ends up with the lion's share of the proceeds. Those who serve in our development office—Julie Randall and Erin DeLullo—worked hard to raise the necessary funding.

Leah and Erin have implemented a comprehensive marketing plan sure to succeed. Chris Ruddy, friend and developer of the hugely successful Internet news magazine www.NewsMax.com, provided encouragement and ideas about how to alert readers about our book. Our new partnership with NewsMax will benefit both organizations.

The public relations firm of Shirley & Banister Public Affairs, headquartered in Old Town Alexandria, Virginia, has been instrumental in the fine points of cover design and title choice. They're working to make the general public aware that the book is in bookstores everywhere. They know how to ensure that my message about the dangerous Hard-Left agenda will be received by as many as possible. Craig Shirley was the public relations expert who helped make *Unlimited Access* a #1 *New York Times* bestseller in 1996, and Craig and Diana and their staff are working very hard on this book to see if we can repeat and even surpass our first success.

Michael Fitterling, graphic artist and editor of Lost Classics Book

Company of Lake Wales, Florida, deserves the credit for polishing a rough manuscript into a work we can be proud of. We're pleased with the attractive, eye-catching, and informative cover he designed. He also located the best printer and coordinated the schedule of printing, and delivery.

Although it's true my family was traumatized by the vicious Clinton administration, they've been very supportive of my new book and understand why I must fight this fight.

Last but not least are the many loyal supporters of The Patrick Henry Center. Without their financial support and encouragement we would not be able to do what we do. All the proceeds from the distribution of this book will go to fund the programs of The Patrick Henry Center. This is the best way I can think of to show that I appreciate the many generous people who have made an investment in my activities and in the Center.